UNBROKEN LIFE

Escape From Abuse & Triumph Over Addiction

Written By Janine Green

Copyrights © 2024

By Janine Green

TXu2-453-911

All Rights Reserved

No part of this book may be reproduced, stored in a retrieval system, or transmitted in any form or by any means electronic, mechanical, photocopy, recording, or otherwise without prior written permission from the author, except for brief quotations in a review. Unauthorized use is strictly prohibited by law.

Table of Contents

Acknowledgments 2

Preface 3

Introduction 4

Chapter One "Meet Molly, AKA Bratnilla" 6

Chapter Two "The Winding Road Ahead" 9

Chapter Three "Boy Crazy-Rebellious" 11

Chapter Four "Who's Your Daddy" 14

Chapter Five "Giving in to the Itch" 18

Chapter Six "Sleeping with the Enemy" 24

Chapter Seven "Cash Cow" 28

Chapter Eight "Strong Premonition" 31

Chapter Nine "Less is More" 36

Chapter Ten "The Beginning of the End" 39

Chapter Eleven "Tattoos and an Heirloom Ring" 42

Chapter Twelve "The Cracks of the Mask" 45

Chapter Thirteen "Barbie and Ken" 48

Chapter Fourteen "Like Father Like Son" 50

Chapter Fifteen "Techno Music and Ecstasy" 53

Chapter Sixteen "Pennies on the Dollars" 57

Chapter Seventeen "Cannon Ball" 60

Chapter Eighteen "Throwing Rocks from a Glass House" ... 64

Chapter Nineteen "Not Around the Kids" 67

Chapter Twenty "Doubled Down" 70

Chapter Twenty-One "Comfortably Numb" 73

Chapter Twenty-Two "The Nightmare had Just Begun" 77

Chapter Twenty-Three "Brass Knuckles and Unfair Fights" 81

Chapter Twenty-Four "A Recipe for Disaster" 84

Chapter Twenty-Five "A Scene from Pulp Fiction" 87

Chapter Twenty-Six "Someone to Blame" 90

Chapter Twenty-Seven "Overzealous Detectives & A Coerced Confession" 94

Chapter Twenty-Eight "The Full Court Press & Unwanted Guest" 98

Chapter Twenty-Nine "Subpoenaed by a Grand Jury" 101

Chapter Thirty "Facing a Potential Life Sentence" 104

Chapter Thirty-One "Shackled to a Gurney" 107

Chapter Thirty-Two "Solitary Confinement- Freedom is an Illusion" . 110

Chapter Thirty-Three "An Unexpected Overnight Visit" 113

Chapter Thirty-Four "The Koala Bear Doesn't Drink" 117

Chapter Thirty-Five "In LIMBO" 121

Chapter Thirty-Six "Judgment Day" 125

Chapter Thirty-Seven "A Trial Visit Turns to Disaster" 129

Chapter Thirty-Eight "The End of Myself" 133

Chapter Thirty-Nine "Strangers Cried with Me" 137

Chapter Forty "Quickly Falling Behind" 141

Chapter Forty-One "I had no Soul Left" 145

Chapter Forty-Two "The Call that Changed My Life" 149

Chapter Forty-Three "Rock Bottom" 152

Chapter Forty-Four "The 14th White Chip-One Last Shot" 157

Chapter Forty-Five "Depression Can't Hit a Moving Target" 160

Chapter Forty-Six "Recovery is about Taking Action" 164

Chapter Forty- Seven "The Great Obsession" 168

Chapter Forty-Eight "Jaded & Rightfully so" 172

Chapter Forty-Nine "A Recycled Phone Number with Profound Messages" 176

Chapter Fifty "Cleaning my Side of the Street" 180

Chapter Fifty-One "The Student Becomes the Teacher" 184

Chapter Fifty-Two "Finding Joy" 188

Chapter Fifty-Three "Daddy's Girl" 191

Chapter Fifty-Four "My Special Boy" 195

Chapter Fifty-Five "My Foot in the Door" 199

Chapter Fifty-Six "Advocating for Adam" 203

Chapter Fifty-Seven "Living Amends" 208

Chapter Fifty-Eight "We were Reborn" 211

Chapter Fifty-Nine "Normies and Earth people" 214

Chapter Sixty "Hope Dealer" 217

*Dedicated To: Alex, Aaron, Danni
Victoria, Shawn, Shalee, and Nijah*

Acknowledgments

My husband David. My precious grandchildren. My mom, siblings, cousins, aunts, and uncles. My friends Teena, Susan, Ally, Tianna, Jackie, Peter, Maureen, Shanna, and Joyce. My sponsees, Kostis P., Larissa M., Arun K. I could not have done any of this without the guidance and direction of my friend Rick B.

Preface

I have wanted to write a book for as long as I can remember. Through the years of being in long-term recovery, I have heard the most amazing stories, the kind that stir your heart! Before developing a problem with alcohol and drugs, I thought addiction was a moral issue. Like many, I looked down on these people that had "lost control". This belief was erroneous.

In my years of sobriety, I have discovered that many people do recover if they can be rigorously honest. These are not bad people trying to get GOOD; they are sick people trying to get WELL. Most everyone on this continent today knows someone, or loves someone, that struggles with an addiction. It might not be alcohol or drugs. It could be gambling, sex & love, online shopping, or food addictions. This "disease" (according to the American Medical Association addiction is a disease) affects millions of people worldwide.

I felt it was very relatable to share Molly's story, with all names changed to protect the innocent. Not only did she get out from abusers and go on to find happiness and healthy relationships; she also overcame an eating disorder. It is after her struggles with addiction that she finds this brand-new way of life and is no longer a victim. My hope is that the radical life changes that she experienced may inspire others who are suffering and feel completely alone. There is hope, and recovery is possible!

Introduction

This is the true story of Molly, who grew up in a rural farming town in upstate New York. Abandoned by her father as a toddler, Molly's mother remarried, providing her with a stable family life during her childhood. However, Molly became pregnant at the young age of 18 years old. After the birth of her daughter, she moved to Oklahoma and married. Her husband, though abusive, was a decent father, and they eventually had a son together.

When the physical abuse extended to their son, Molly packed up her kids and left. With no education or marketable skills, she became an adult entertainer, as it was the only immediate way to support her two young children without receiving any child support.

One summer, Molly's cousin came to visit, bringing along some friends. One of them, whom we'll call Donnie, had a crush on Molly, and the feeling was mutual. They quickly fell into a whirlwind romance that lasted just three months. Living over a thousand miles apart, they would meet in different cities, staying in fancy hotels. But much later, Molly discovered that Don had been playing a role all along, only showing her the version of himself that he knew she would love.

After a whirlwind ninety-day romance, Molly and Donnie ran off to Las Vegas and got married. They would eventually move to Tampa, Florida, where Don had been living. It quickly became clear that her new husband was addicted to alcohol and drugs. Despite this, Molly tried to make the marriage work. Then came the emotional and physical abuse. She kept telling herself it wasn't as bad as her first marriage. What happened next, however, would become a nightmare for her and her entire family.

This book is about a woman who succumbs to addiction after surviving trauma and extensive abuse. She is in a fight for her life. Eventually, she prevails and puts the pieces of her life back together. After turning her life around, she goes on to help thousands of other suffering people.

Chapter One
"Meet Molly, AKA Bratnilla"

I was born in a little town in New York called Warsaw. My parents were very young and newly married. Both of my parents worked in a Motorola factory but neither made much money. According to the stories I was told later in life, my father was already struggling with substance abuse. Right before Christmas, my father stole from mom's slender purse. This was just one of many similar instances. I was only a toddler when he left us and started a new life.

I didn't have any memories of my dad until I was four years old. I remember going to stay with him and his newest girlfriend; she had two young boys of her own. We were in Pennsylvania, and I was so excited to spend time with my dad. I didn't see much of him while I was there because he was working, and I became bedridden with a bad case of poison ivy.

Most of my childhood memories are of my cousins, my grandparents, my aunts, and my mom. I was always the kid that didn't have a dad around. I think my grandma worked hard to make sure to give me special attention and even showed me favoritism at times. Mom would do or buy almost anything I asked for as well. I became somewhat of a spoiled child and my favorite aunt called me "Bratnilla."

My mother had to work tirelessly to care for me, as my father did not provide any child support. We lived in trailers, small apartments, and run-down houses. She frequently went out on dates, seeking a father figure or someone to assist her in raising me. There were a couple of failed relationships, even one man who abused me. I never held my mother responsible for any of this; it was always his fault! If my father had been involved in any way, even if it was just for financial support, most of this situation would have been avoided.

I remember mom and I had this cool apartment in Arcade, NY when I was 9 years old. I had a bicycle that I loved to ride everywhere I went. I was often home alone, but sometimes grandma would come to stay with me. When my mom was home, we were so happy. She tried her hand at dating again. I remember waking up one night and some strange man was staring at me while I was asleep in my bed.

Then something seemed to change. She met a man named Phil who appeared to be quite decent. The most exciting aspect was that Phil had three small children of his own, and we were set to become a family unit. I had been an only child for 9 years of my lonely life. Every time I threw a penny in the wishing well, every time I blew out the candles on my cake, I always wished for the same thing, to have a dad. Now it seemed I was getting not only a father but also some siblings. I was thrilled!

The transition was not an easy one. By this time, I had become quite self-centered and accustomed to getting my own way. This new dad was strict. I remember the first time we had dinner at his house; he made me eat all my vegetables. I was very angry and began pouting, so I had to sit at the dinner table for hours until I finished every bite. In addition to being strict, he was also very kind to me and to my mother.

Suddenly, I was the oldest of four kids, and I took that role very seriously. I loved playing with my little sisters. My brother was very sweet and quiet. Soon after, they tied the knot and welcomed their first child. We had a true mixed family—his, hers, and ours.

Phil was a dairy farmer with his brothers. We welcomed numerous new cousins, aunts, and uncles into our circle. Large family celebrations and holidays were the best. Mom's family blended very well with our new family. Eventually, my stepfather formally adopted me and gave me his last name; we all had the same last name, and I really felt like I belonged.

I was the oldest sibling and felt responsible to protect, love, and guide my younger siblings. Our childhood wasn't perfect. I did not know many of the things that were going on and still didn't fully understand. What I do know is that we were loved. We had clothes, and we got to participate in dance class, cheerleading, and hockey for my brothers. No family is ever perfect. I will not trash talk about my parents; they are human. I have made just as many, if not more, mistakes with my own kids than they did with us. There is no handbook that comes with instructions on how to not make mistakes as parents. Whatever has happened in the past, I have forgiven. I pray that each of my siblings can find their own path to forgiveness.

Chapter Two

"The Winding Road Ahead"

From kindergarten to 3rd grade, we relocated frequently. I attended three different schools in that short time. I never really set down roots, and it was hard to make good long-term friends; I was always the new girl. That all changed once mom, and I finally had a family of our own.

We rode the bus to school in Holland, NY, from our small farming town of Strykersville. This was a very rural area. Our bus ride to and from school was close to an hour each way. We had fun on the bus. Some kids were teased more than others, though. I remember there was a sweet boy named Shawn who was teased the most. Shawn was always attempting to fit in, and one day, the other boys encouraged him to play a prank on me. Right before Shawn got off the bus, he yanked my pants down to my ankles, almost everyone was laughing. I didn't laugh, and neither did Shawn. I will never forget the look on his face.

Even though I never would hold it against him, I could tell that he really regretted what he did to me. I was a good sport; I knew they had pushed him to do it. When he apologized to me days later, I told him that I forgave him. After a few more weeks, I remember riding the bus to school and waiting for him to arrive in the driveway, but he wasn't there. Shawn usually waited outside when we pulled up, or he would rush out quickly. I will never forget that day. The bus driver waited and waited and even honked the horn.

I'm not sure how much time passed but finally, we left without him. We went to the end of that road, picked up those kids, and turned around, but there was still no sign of him.

That evening after school, I remember my parents whispering and talking in hushed tones. They called me downstairs and sat me at the kitchen table. I remember dad saying to me, "Molly, do you remember a boy named Shawn, a boy that was in school a year ahead of you?" I responded, "Of course I do." He told me, "Sometime this morning after you left for school, he grabbed a gun, went to the shed in his parents' yard, and committed suicide."

I was mortified. I could not believe the words coming out of his mouth. How many times had I ridden to school sitting next to him, laughing and talking all the way? How many deep conversations did we have on those rides home, especially when the other boys weren't around? This was the first time that someone close to me, someone I knew personally, had died. And at his own hands. To this day, I wonder if maybe we had waited a few more minutes… maybe he was in the shed right then trying to get up the nerve to pull the trigger? Death is so final.

Chapter Three
"Boy Crazy-Rebellious"

My high school years weren't terrible. I was, what I would call, popular. Not the most popular by any means, but I had lots of friends and at least one very good friend that I shared everything with. Her name was Lynn. Lynn was the only friend my parents trusted, so we spent a lot of time together, either at her house or mine.

My parents were overprotective and extremely strict with me during my teenage years. I am sure it didn't help that I was "boy crazy". Looking back, I believe my mother wanted me to avoid the same mistakes she had made. Having me so young and being stuck in that loveless marriage, not going to college directly after high school, always struggling to get by; she wanted to protect me from a life like that.

The more rules they gave me, the more rebellious I became. I remember kids in high school asking me "What time is your curfew?" I would answer "I don't have a curfew." Most of them would say how cool that must be. Regrettably, it was anything but cool. I didn't have a curfew because I wasn't allowed out at all. Additionally, if I made a mistake or lied to my parents, instead of grounding me for a week or weekend, they would ground me for 2 or 3 months.

I was never allowed to go to the Boys and Girls club. I am not sure why, but I just wasn't given permission. Everybody I knew would go hang out there. They would play games, they would kiss boys, they would dance, and I was jealous, because I couldn't join them. This really ate me up, and eventually, I made up this story that I was going to hang out with my best friend at her house. Instead, I went to a dance at the Boys' club. A few days later, my dad came home from the farm, and he cornered me in the kitchen and asked me, where did I go on Friday night? Of course, I told him a lie. That was the only time in my entire life that he ever slapped me, straight across the face. "Never lie to me," he said.

I will say this: my parents' guidance and their rules did assist me in a few areas. For one thing, I did get pretty good grades and eventually graduated from high school. Secondly, I was not smoking pot or drinking as a teenager. I agree that things could have been much worse for me during those challenging years if not for their strict rules.

I had several different boyfriends during high school. One of the main boys that I cared for was Jimmy. Jimmy, who was a year ahead of me in school, had already realized that his parents couldn't afford to send him to college, and he had no desire to take out student loans. Jimmy joined the military, so for most of my senior year, I was alone. We had already gotten an apartment of our own before he went to basic training.

I worked part time at a gas station and occasionally skipped school. Within months of him leaving for basic training, I found out that I was pregnant. I was a teenager. I had a hard time figuring out if it was Jimmy's or if it was my new boyfriend, Darryl's.

Darryl moved into the apartment with me. He clearly had some type of drinking problem. He couldn't hold down a job at all. Every night, he would frequent bars or attend keg parties with his friends. I resented all of this. Here I was still trying to graduate from high school, battling morning sickness and doctor appointments, and paying the bills.

One evening, when I was particularly exhausted (from being pregnant and going to work) one of my friends called our apartment. She asked me if I knew where my boyfriend was, and I said no, that I didn't. She said I needed to see this for myself. My friend came and picked me up; she took me to a birthday party that was in a barn. This family, consisting of numerous teenagers, appeared to have few rules and frequently hosted parties. I was still confused as to why she brought me here. My friend led me through the barn and into a large room filled with hay bales, where I first saw him. My boyfriend, the father of my baby, was being intimate with another girl, and I caught them in the act. Watching him do it with another girl, that wasn't me, made me want to throw up!

After my friend drove me home, I went to retrieve my money. I still didn't have quite enough for rent, but I had a couple of hundred dollars saved. I checked the drawer where I had left the cash, only to find it gone. Darryl was the only person who had access to or knowledge of where the money was kept. Not only had he been cheating on me, but he also stole from me. I finally understood what my mom was trying to protect me from. After that incident, I had enough of being on my own and went crawling back to my parents' home with my tail between my legs.

Chapter Four
"Who's Your Daddy"

The day that I turned 18 years old, my long-lost father called me. I am guessing that he got my phone number from one of my aunts. I answered the phone, and not recognizing his voice asked, "Who is this?" He responded, "It's your dad." I responded, "No, that's not true." He said, "Yes, it's your real dad." I was angry when I learned that he had been living an hour away from me for several years but waited until he was no longer financially obligated to call. On the other hand, strange as it may sound, I had been longing to know him all my life. I had always felt like something was missing.

My father's name was Daniel, but most people called him Danny. He asked me if I wanted to meet him that weekend, but I declined, stating that I had been waiting for many years. I said, " If you want to meet me, then I want to see you today." We met at a McDonald's halfway between where he and I lived. I said on the phone, "How will I know who you are?" He said, "I will have on painting clothes and a hat." I walked into that restaurant with my heart pounding and palms sweating. I figured out which man he was and sat down at the table with him. He lit a cigarette. I reached into my purse and grabbed my own cigarettes. I remember him opening his mouth as he began to lecture me about smoking. I quickly snapped and told him, "I don't think you will get to tell me what or what not to do." "Fair enough," he said. We ate some food and talked for a long time; I shared my life story with him and asked him a few questions of my own.

My father had fallen in love with a local girl, and she had a beautiful teenage daughter of her own. Malinda, her daughter, was several years younger than me; but we hit it off right from the start. I started to spend time with my father and his new family, this happened around the time of my early pregnancy. When my relationship with Darryl began to deteriorate due to his cheating and theft, my father unexpectedly intervened and turned things around. He even replaced the two hundred dollars missing from my rent.

When I moved back into my parents' home, I still stayed in touch with my father and his new family. They would go on family vacations initially, and they would invite me along. I loved this. I was really enjoying getting to know my biological father after all those years of dreaming about him. The only problem was that even from the start, his new wife could not stand me. As time went by, I would come visit on the weekends, and they would be looking at photos of family vacations that they took, without me. They even brought some of their buddies on these trips; that I wasn't even aware of. I was so hurt. It seemed like the closer I came to him, the more his wife became less tolerant of me. I would make every effort to ensure that I wasn't being a burden and made sure I cleaned up after myself. I was always polite and passive. Nothing worked. She made it obvious that she couldn't stand me.

When I was further along in my pregnancy and starting to show, it was time for my high school graduation. I was 3 credits short because of my absenteeism from being sick while pregnant. They allowed me to still walk across that stage with my empty diploma with the rest of my senior class. My parents, grandparents, and father were all there. It was such a happy day for me.

My parents were adamant about me making up those credits and getting my actual diploma since to them a GED was unacceptable. One of my aunts found St. Mary's school for pregnant, unwed mothers, and they signed me up. I did not know what to expect. This was a school that young ladies lived in. I thought maybe it was where the Catholics hid their teenage pregnant daughters.

I packed my clothes and toiletries and went. Although I wasn't a heavy smoker at the time, I enjoyed smoking cigarettes and was apprehensive that I might not be able to do so now that I was heading there. I couldn't have been more wrong about that though. They had a smoking room in the building. There were probably 10 of us, and all the girls, except for one, were smokers. We would listen to music, sing, dance, tell stories, and smoke together. It was a lot of fun. I formed some deep, lasting bonds with some of these women.

We took our classes during the day. I had missed too many gym classes, so one of my requirements was exercise. They surprisingly had a pregnancy aerobics and dance class for us several times per week. And oh, how I loved to dance. From the age of nine, I studied jazz, tap, and ballet classes for almost a decade. Dancing gave me so much joy; it even gave me an escape from whatever fears and worries I had.

I was full of fear. Would I lose my father again after finally getting him back in my life? Would I ever be in a decent relationship, one where I'm not cheated on and stole from? Should I try again with Darryl? Jimmy still loved me and was calling me all the time; at least he was stable. He had his military career and at the time we didn't know that the baby I was carrying wasn't his; we didn't find that out until she was a teenager. I feared that staying in New York would confine me to the limited opportunities in that small town. I decided at the time to just focus on having a healthy baby and on enriching my relationship with all three of my parents. My siblings and I also became quite close during my pregnancy.

Chapter Five
"Giving in to the Itch"

During my first pregnancy, nobody told me about stretch marks or how to prevent them. There were so many things I didn't know about childbirth, pregnancy, or parenting. I had so many fears. I wanted to do everything right. I wanted my daughter to have the world and everything in it.

I never told Darryl that I saw him that night in the barn with that strange girl. I assumed he would likely deny it. I was confident that there had been other women as well. I was a few years younger than him, but I wasn't stupid. I was almost positive that the baby inside me was his. There were several times during the pregnancy that I would go back to him and try to make it work for our daughter. I wanted her to have a father that I never had. This desire for her left me vulnerable to all kinds of crappy behaviors from him.

I stayed with him for about a month at his parents' house. He was one of six kids, and the house was pretty full, so we slept on a cot in the basement together. I felt like an outsider. They were nice, but not very friendly. I could see the pity in their eyes when they looked at me. I wasn't working at this time, so I was totally dependent on him. Unfortunately, he wasn't any good at holding down a job back then. His siblings would get him a job, but as soon as payday came, he would be out at the bars. Sometimes he didn't come home for days. It was very awkward living in the basement at that time. Even when he was home with me, he was almost always drunk. One night, while I was asleep, I woke up to a strange sound. I sat up on the cot and saw him standing in the corner of the basement taking a leak. There was no toilet down there. He was just so inebriated he thought he was in the bathroom.

I would cry all the time. I would take long hot baths, pour water over my belly and tell my little girl all about what her life was going to be like. Long before she was born, she was already the most significant relationship in my life. When I visited the doctor in my second trimester, he diagnosed me with chlamydia and crabs. I was stunned. I was embarrassed and very hurt. I was in love with him, or at least the idea of him. During this appointment, they informed me of the presence of abnormal cells on my uterus and recommended a medical abortion. They explained to me that if it was cancer, then it would get exponentially worse by the time I gave birth. According to the doctors, pregnancy would be a fertilized area for anything to grow.

I would not even consider it. First, we did not know if it was cancer or not. Second, by now I can feel my baby move every day, and I have already fallen in love with her. In my opinion, there was only one option, and that was for me to have my baby. Of course, I still had to take the antibiotics, apply this unpleasant smelling cleansing shampoo, and use a comb to remove the crabs. What type of man deceives his girlfriend while she is pregnant? What kind of man gives her sexually transmitted diseases as well? Very few people were aware of the depth of betrayal I was facing. I had my baby, and I had my pride. I just kept going. I put one foot in front of the other and held my head high.

Remember my high school sweetheart, Jimmy? He continued to reach out to me. After this medical incident, I moved back in with my parents and siblings. Jimmy was doing well in the Air Force. As soon as he was able, he came to visit me. I was about 7 months pregnant and big in every way. He didn't care. He found me very attractive, and he made sure that I felt special and beautiful. We went to a hotel and stayed overnight; this was all while I was living in the Catholic home. We were allowed to leave on the weekends. We ate at a nice restaurant and talked for hours. He held me in his arms and whispered promises in my ears. He would rub my belly, get down on his knees, and speak to the baby. He not only had a job; he had his own apartment, a vehicle, good credit—everything you would want in a husband.

Jimmy returned to Oklahoma, where he was stationed. I stayed in New York with my parents but lived in the pregnancy home during the week. I remember fondly the weekends when my father picked me up from school and took me grocery shopping. He would tease and try to mimic me as I waddled down the aisles of the store because I had gotten so big. He didn't do it to hurt my feelings, I'm sure it looked strange, this tiny young girl with a large belly.

While living at the Catholic school for unwed mothers, I did receive some counseling and therapy. I had experienced abandonment and even some abuse. I wanted to make sure that I could protect her from anything and everything. I was a baby having a baby. I got so big, I was enormous. My abdomen was covered with extensive purple-red stretch marks. I would spend hours digging my nails into my skin and giving in to the itch as my skin kept spreading further than it was ever meant to.

I was due on New Year's Eve that year, but this baby did not want to come out. I had a regular full-term doctor's appointment that morning. They did the usual exam and said that I was almost 4 cm dilated already. I didn't feel anything yet. I went back to pregnancy school, which had a full medical staff on site; and there I labored. I smoked a cigarette and even took a nap. The next time they checked, I was already 6cm dilated, and it was time to take me to Mercy Hospital. My mother was with me, but my best friend Lynn had been my "Lamaze partner," and she was the one I thought I had to have with me, she had just had a baby herself.

My mom called my best friend, who was at work. I think I remember her telling my mom that first labor takes a long time. She was confident that she could complete her shift before the baby arrived. My doctor was attending the Buffalo Sabres game. The nurses called, and he said not to worry; he would get back in plenty of time to help me deliver. I listened as my mother tried to warn them that if I was anything like her, then this was going to happen quickly. Nobody believed that, but mom was right.

It only felt like I had mild cramps. Soon after arriving at the hospital though, I felt the first bit of pain. I started begging for an epidural or some type of pain medication. The nurse did another check and said sorry, it's too late now. I was already 10cm dilated, and the medicine would never have time to kick in if they administered it then. They called my doctor from the hockey game; he arrived just in the nick of time. As soon as they told me to push, I did. I pushed two more times, and she was out.

It is amazing how God made our bodies work. After giving birth to my precious, healthy baby girl, I then had to deliver the placenta. I was unaware that this occurs in every vaginal birth. It just so happens that bringing my baby to full term may have very well saved my life. Remember the abnormal, possibly cancerous, cells found on my uterus? They shed during the placenta delivery. The entire uterine wall came out, cells and all! To me, this was a miracle.

Nowadays, only a small number of women undergo natural childbirth, and while I would have gladly taken medication to ease the pain, I'm grateful that I didn't. What they don't tell you is that your brain is flooded with endorphins when you give birth naturally. This must be why in the old days before epidurals, women still had multiple children. Otherwise, that extreme pain would have deterred them from ever giving birth more than once. I was elated; that is the best word I could use to describe how I was feeling.

After holding my precious, healthy, beautiful girl, it was time to give her a name. We had tried every number we could call, but no one could reach Darryl to tell him. His sister answered and told my mom she knew he shouldn't have gone to the strip joint in Canada this late in the pregnancy, but that is where he was. I was shockingly calm as my revenge plan began to form. Her birth certificate carries no mention of his name. I named her Rose and gave her my last name.

Over the next six weeks, I played a role and was very nice to him. Whenever he wanted to see his daughter, I would make her and myself available. We went camping with friends of his, we listened to live bands, and we kissed often. He was always showing off his baby girl. He was holding her in almost every picture. I secured a job as a waitress and began earning my own money. I was also exercising and eating healthier. I quickly got down to my pre-baby weight, and I was really feeling myself. He was totally into me. What he didn't know was that all that he had done to me when I was most vulnerable, he could not undo.

I went to my six-week doctor's checkup and got the all-clear to have an intimate sexual life again. I picked out a sensual outfit and invited him over. My parents were out of town, and I had the house to myself. I cooked him dinner, and we made love in front of the fireplace and put our daughter to bed. The perfect evening was coming to an end, and he had no idea what lay ahead.

My biological father understood that I could not stay in New York. I would never have a decent life, and neither would Rose.

Jimmy had invited us to live in Oklahoma with him. He offered to take care of both of us. I could even stay home and not work if I wanted to. I wanted my daughter to have a dad. A man who could hold down a job—even a career. I wanted her to have a stay-at-home mother who could care for her every day. This was it, our only shot at a "real" life.

Before the enchanted evening with Darryl, I gave a picture to his friend's girlfriend and told her what I was going to do. I knew she felt bad for him, but she was willing to keep my secret. She knew what a dog he had been to me during the whole pregnancy. The picture was of him holding his daughter. On the back it said, "You screwed me, now I screwed you!" The next day, as we embarked on our journey to a new life in Oklahoma, I boarded a Greyhound bus with our baby, and she presented him with the picture. I did not see him or speak to him again for many years. My sister ran into him at a car race, many years later; she said he still had that picture in his wallet. In my book, that was the ultimate revenge.

Chapter Six
"Sleeping with the Enemy"

My beautiful little baby and I rode on that Greyhound bus for nearly 24 hours. It was a long ride, which gave me plenty of time to think about everything that had happened. My parents, especially my mother, were upset with me for moving their grandchild across the country. I felt terrible about the pain that I was causing them. They didn't understand the depth of the betrayal that I had endured.

Jimmy and I settled into a quiet life together. He was enamored with baby Rose. It didn't matter to him whether she was his biological daughter, but he didn't want to take a test to find out. He loved her so much. He was a wonderful father to her. In his eyes, she could do nothing wrong. He was a good provider, and I was finally able to stay home full time and be her mommy. That was the most important thing to me.

Soon after arriving in Oklahoma, he asked me to marry him. We moved to Del City in February, and in March we went to the courthouse to get married. I was only 19 years old. Right from the beginning of the marriage, there was abuse. My new husband had a severe case of obsessive-compulsive disorder. If the dishes weren't done right, if the towel hanging in the bathroom had a stain on it, if anything was out of place, he would lose his temper. He would call me mean names. He yelled at me often. He would squeeze my wrists. He would push me down onto the floor or even step on my bare feet while wearing his combat boots. He wasn't hitting me or punching me, not at first, but he was certainly abusing me.

He was so happy and loving with our daughter that I decided to skip a couple of birth control pills, thinking another baby might get him to treat me a little better. Especially because this would be his biological child for sure. It didn't take long before I became pregnant again. Initially he was upset about it, but he came around. Rose was super excited about being a big sister.

We firmly believed that our first apartment harbored ghosts. It was a 2-bedroom townhouse. When we had guests over, I would set up the baby monitor downstairs while the baby slept upstairs. Almost every time we could hear a woman singing lullabies to the baby. We had another military couple that came over and played cards with us. They would also witness some of these strange events. Eventually, we moved to a bigger apartment, one that didn't have any ghosts.

As soon as I started to show in my pregnancy, Jimmy started going out on the weekends and even during the week. He was always infatuated with very thin women and would constantly insult and compare me to them. I was falling apart emotionally. I had already been through hell with Darryl; I did not want to be in that situation again. I was able to endure the abuse because it was solely directed towards me. But Jimmy going to the strip clubs all the time while I was pregnant was a hard pill to swallow.

There was an incident, at night, when I took his car keys from him. I was crying my eyes out. Big and pregnant with his son, I begged him to please stay home with me. He pushed me hard. I fell on the ground outside in the parking lot. This did not deter him; he was the man, and he was going out. I could tell he had very little concern for my feelings. Sometimes when he came home, he would tell me all about this stripper or that one. He would describe to me the extra show they would give him, because he was so charming. He would also describe in detail how amazing their bodies were. A couple of times he tried talking me into having extramarital affairs with him and other people, but I was not interested.

Once when I was about 7 months pregnant, he did not come home at all. What a nightmare. I thought he was going to be so different. Here I had uprooted our lives to come here and have a fresh start only to end up in the very same boat all over again. I felt like such a fool. When he returned home the next afternoon, he acted like it was no big deal. He had gone out to a club with his friend's ex-girlfriend and then claimed he was too drunk to drive home. Those two had always had chemistry between them, that I could see. I was almost positive that he had cheated on me. He just told me to shut my mouth and stop asking questions. I became very depressed during this time. If it wasn't for Rose and the baby in my belly, I don't know what I would have done. I clearly had terrible taste in men.

In May of that year, I gave birth to a beautiful, healthy son, and we named him Adam. He was a very fussy baby right from the start. Only 16 months separated him from Rose. I was a stay-at-home babysitter by this time. I enjoyed watching other people's kids, and it gave me a little money of my own. I didn't leave because I truly enjoyed being a stay-at-home mom with my own children.

The abuse began to escalate a little bit at a time. The verbal abuse was the worst. The bruises would heal much quicker than the emotions would. Some things you say to a person you can never take back. I always told myself he was a good provider and a good father. I promised myself that I could take it; I would stay as long as he never touched the kids.

It was during this time in my life that I developed an eating disorder called anorexia nervosa. The more weight I lost, the more attractive he found me. It wasn't about food for me; it was about control. When Adam was four months old, I ended up in the emergency room. I had a fever of over 104 degrees. I had to drive myself to the hospital. He didn't believe me when I told him I was sick. I had tunnel vision while I was driving and still don't know how I made it there in one piece. The hospital quickly diagnosed me with full blown pneumonia. I remember hearing the doctors discussing my case while I was in and out of it from the fever. I clearly heard them say something about end-stage anorexia. I had hair all over my arms called lanugo. Apparently, when people starve themselves for a long period of time, they grow this hair so that the body can help moderate its temperature.

Our home life was hell sometimes and dreamy at others. I didn't have any skills. I had no support system out there and I had no desire to return to New York. So, I stayed, and I put up with it, day in and day out. I kept my head up; I even joined a local church, and the whole family would go together, which gave me renewed hope.

Chapter Seven

"Cash Cow"

The thing about an abusive relationship is that you can't just leave overnight. You have to plan and be ready long before the incident that finally breaks you enough to leave. While my husband was TDY (temporary duty station) and months before I left him, I was already beginning my exit plan. The thing about abusers is: If you stay after the abuse begins, it will almost always escalate over time. The mental and physical torture were progressively getting worse, and I knew the time would come when I would have to leave.

I always resented how much time and money he wasted on the strip joints. To me, it felt very much like he was having an affair. Jimmy even admitted to me that he occasionally fantasized about these women while he was making love to me. This was just another form of mental abuse. The smaller he made me feel, the more dependent I was on him.

In case something worse happened, I had to figure out a way to become independent. There was no way out for me. Nevertheless, I needed to prepare myself in case the day came when he hurt the kids. Therefore, during his absence, I entrusted my friends with the children's care, while I actively sought employment. I had applied for jobs all over the Oklahoma City area. Retail stores, restaurants, and even an optical place. I had no education and no skills. They offered bare minimum pay that would never allow me to support myself.

That's when the thought occurred to me... The one thing that I was great at was dancing. All those years of dance lessons. In high school, I was a competitive tap dancer and made music with my feet. Despite his attempts to undermine my self-esteem, I was still considered young and attractive. Even though he made sure that I didn't see myself this way. There were many men and women in my life who told me I was beautiful and that I deserved better. Most of these people were his own friends.

That's when I went to a strip club and applied to be a waitress or bartender. Jimmy was out of the country working for a few weeks. The manager at the club said, "No, sweetheart, we don't have any of those positions available." As I was walking away, he said, "But I would love to hire you". I said, "What is the job"? He told me to get on that stage and dance to see if it's something you could do.

My thinking at the time was this...I am unsure if I can leave my husband; perhaps he will realize that he does not wish to share me with other men if I begin stripping. Maybe he will turn it around and realize that a married man should be at home with his wife and kids. So, the following day, I returned to the club, dressed in high heels and a sexy outfit.

Back in the early 90's the Oklahoma/ Texas area was considered the Bible belt. There wasn't any nudity; there were no friction lap dances. Ladies wore full bottoms and pasties covering their nipples. They didn't perform lap dances; instead, they performed table dances directly in front of the customers. This was an upscale adult entertainment establishment with lots of old oil money.

I worked four shifts that first week and cleared $1,500 after tipping out the DJ, the bartender, and the door guys. I felt empowered. My self-esteem was already halfway to where it had been before my marriage. I worked at night while the kids were asleep, and I had plenty of money to do whatever they wanted during the day. This was not my ideal situation, but it provided a solution.

I couldn't wait for him to return home. I just knew in my heart that he would demand that I stop dancing. I was even hopeful that I had some negotiating tools, and that he would now also stay at home. The strip joint phase would be behind us at long last.

To my utter shock, this was not to be. I informed Jimmy that I had been stripping for three weeks while he was away. I braced myself, envisioning a knockdown drag-out fight that would leave me covered in bruises. Instead, he smiled broadly and extended his arms. He enveloped me in an embrace and expressed his enthusiastic approval, stating "This is fantastic." He proceeded to tell me about all the sexy stripper friends I would make, and the extra cash he would now have for tipping them. He even dared to suggest that he might finally achieve the extramarital affair he had always yearned for.

This was the beginning of the end for me. Clearly, my husband had no respect for me whatsoever. Each night when I dragged myself home from the club, he would take my bags and start counting out all the dollar bills. He made stacks of 20's, 5's, 1's, 10's, and even 100's. He had a calendar and would write the total amount of my take so we could look at it all the time. My new nickname was Cash Cow. The expectation was always for me to make more. As I improved and started to double what I had made, he called me Cash Cow Squared!

Chapter Eight

"Strong Premonition"

During my initial months as an adult entertainer, I received unwavering admiration at home. That was how he made me feel at the time. It was like, for the first time ever, Jimmy respected me. Things appeared to be improving.

We began looking for a new home. I had my eye on a beautiful 2-story custom-built home in Moore, OK. This home was in a great school district. There was a lush carpet and beautiful hardwood floors. When you walked through the front door, there was a gorgeous crystal chandelier. In addition to a formal dining room, there was an eat-in kitchen with a built-in oak table with benches and matching cabinets. There was a 2nd living room upstairs with 3 bedrooms and another bathroom. The spacious master bedroom was located downstairs, complete with his and her walk-in closets.

I had never been in a more beautiful home. I am grateful that right from the beginning Jimmy did teach me how to build my credit, and I paid taxes on my self-employed business. I am not sure how much I made that first year, but I paid taxes on 150K. In 1993 that was a lot of money, especially for someone barely over the age of 20.

We needed $25k for a down payment on the loan for that house. Even though we had a safe full of cash, it had to be money the bank could track. He had previously purchased a brand-new GMC Sierra extended cab pickup with the money I earned during my first year, we bought it out right with cash. Then we took out a loan against his truck to use for the downpayment of our new home. I borrowed some money from a good friend that I had made in the club, and then we bought that house.

I made new friends at work. These were not merely acquaintances, but women who genuinely cared for and looked out for each other. It took a while for me to open up to anyone. Initially, I didn't want any of them to dislike my husband, as I was uncertain about my ability to leave the marriage. My new job seemed to have pulled us closer together. Despite being a terrible husband, he was a decent father. That held a lot of weight for me.

I will never forget the excitement. Moving into our new home was literally a dream come true. The rooms were so big that the furniture we had looked like doll furniture inside this house. We began shopping at all the name-brand furniture stores. We selected a superior quality California King Sleigh bed, complemented by matching granite top dressers and mirrored armoire. We did the same thing for our living room, dining room, and the kid's rooms. Prior to this, we only had used furniture.

When our son was 4 years old, we were in the kitchen when my husband started shoving me around. On this day, my son decided to protect his mom. He was a tiny little thing. He stood between his father and me and raised his hands. He put up his little fists and said, "If you want to hit my mom, you will have to go thru me." At that moment, my husband lost his temper, striking one of our children for the first time in his life. He got him really good. The knobs on the lower cabinets were at eye level with our son. That quick little beating did a lot of damage. Soon after, it was time for Jimmy to leave for work. I could tell he felt bad. I could see for the first time; he was genuinely afraid that I might leave. I told him the same things I had in the past, the things I knew he needed to hear to get him out of the house. "I know you didn't mean to do it.

I know you are very sorry. I believe you that it will never happen again." Every battered woman reading this will know what I am talking about. He would always feel this terrible remorse. He would make all the promises, and he probably even meant them, but he just couldn't help himself. I knew if I stayed, it was only going to get worse.

When he finally left for work, I packed up all the important documents, the kids, and the essentials. One of the ladies that I babysat for, her husband was a military police officer. I went to their house; they took photos. I filed for a divorce and a restraining order the next day. The restraining order was granted immediately, and the divorce came soon after. The MP started a report on the Air Force base, and my husband was asked to leave the military quietly. Otherwise, he was looking at a dishonorable discharge for what he had done to our son.

The incident with my son in the kitchen occurred shortly after we moved into our new dream home. I remember taking a bath with both of my children in the garden tub in the master bathroom. My daughter could tell that I was scared. I asked them this question; "How would you guys feel if we didn't live with Daddy anymore?" "What if it was only you and mommy?" Neither of them hesitated, "we want to be with you" they both said.

Unfortunately, I was already renting our first home, the one we had just moved out of, to a stripper who was paying us more than we could have gotten by selling it. The rent she paid was almost covering the mortgage on the second house.

I wanted Jimmy out. I had made my decision when I filed for divorce and got the restraining order. I was done for good. And thanks to his practical insistence that I keep dancing, I could easily support myself and the kids with plenty left over. I opened my first ever bank account in my name. I owned a new car and had a safe brimming with cash.

Jimmy was a tough negotiator though and wasn't going to let me off that easily. When I filed for divorce, we worked out the details together. Neither one of us wanted all the money going to lawyers. We set up a plan where I paid for his deposit and the first 6 months of rent at a nearby apartment. I also purchased all the new furniture throughout. He was struggling to make his truck payment, and that money was already invested in the newly purchased house I was living in with the kids.

I would drop the kids off on the weekend, and he would bring them home Sunday evening before school. Everything seemed quite amicable initially.

My mom unexpectedly called me one day. She sounded frightened and said, "Molly, whatever you do, don't let Jimmy in the house." I thought she was crazy and way overreacting. "Mom, we've already resolved everything; he is aware that it's over. We haven't had a single argument since he moved out" I replied. There are some things that science can't explain, and premonition is one of them.

That very same evening, I had already put the kids to bed. I was downstairs in the living room drinking a glass of wine and writing checks to pay the bills. It was late. I could hear what sounded like a storm coming. There was a knock on my front door.

I went to the door and looked out. It was Jimmy, and he was smiling at me. I didn't even hesitate to open it. I stepped on the front step and asked, "What's up?" He glanced back at his truck, revealing a smashed side window. He explained to me what had happened. He was at a strip club when someone smashed his truck window. He said "I just need a plastic bag and some tape in case it starts raining."

I stepped aside and allowed him into the house. He turned and locked the door behind him, and that's when I saw the rifle in his hands. I saw the evil in his eyes as he slowly pushed me back into my bedroom. He began to threaten me, saying that if I didn't follow his instructions, he would kill me, and the kids would discover my body.

He ordered me to take off my pants. I knew right then that he intended to rape me. He set the gun down and pushed me onto the floor. I had tight jeans on. He would push them down a few inches, and I would wiggle them back up. I was not about to let him rape me. This struggle went on for a few more minutes. I pushed past him, and he fell to the ground. I grabbed the phone and ran. I then called 911. While I was on the phone with the operator, we heard the gun go off. Jimmy had threatened suicide many times prior. He had locked my bedroom door and was barricaded inside. The room was completely silent. The cops were still far from the house. A few seconds later, he came running through the house and out to his truck. I stayed on the line until the police arrived. The cops were still in the house when dispatch said they had pulled him over in his truck. Apparently, he had already disassembled his gun. They didn't want to exacerbate his difficult situation any worse, so they simply placed him in the drunk tank for the night. I made sure after that to never let him get close to me again. It was only by God's grace that I hadn't been raped or killed. Mom was right after all.

Chapter Nine

"Less is More"

This next period, looking back, was the best years of my kid's childhood. They were in kindergarten and first grade. We were together all the time. I am delighted that during this period, I lavished them with gifts. Not just with material things, but with my time.

I was happily single and not looking to date. I had several close girlfriends; some of them stayed the night at my house regularly. I also had a handful of great guy friends, totally platonic in nature. I loved these people, and they became our family. You can't choose your family, but you can choose to love certain people for eternity, and these are those friends.

Two of my dearest friends, Ray and Jeff, moved upstairs and paid rent. Adam was having night terrors all the time and slept in my bed almost exclusively. Rose was my only independent child who slept in her own room.

She had a queen-sized, grown-up, solid oak poster bed with matching nightstands and dressers. Her room looked like a Barbie castle. One of my "regulars" from the club owned a large toy store out of state and whenever an exclusive Barbie or other new toy came on the market, he would bring it for my kids.

We did everything together. The beauty of the industry that I worked in was that I could go into the club whenever I wanted. I typically worked four nights a week and only while they were asleep. If my roommate/friend Ray wasn't watching them, then my elderly neighbor was down the road. My kids were happy. They were polite, well mannered, and got along with everyone.

We went to the circus. We went to the Zoo. We traveled. I took them to Disney on Ice and every year to the state fair. I'll never forget my first summer when I was single. The kids and I went to the fair almost every day. It was extremely hot that year. My backyard wasn't big enough for a pool. However, they had large, gorgeous hot tubs and custom enclosures on display, and we were interested in purchasing one.

Rose and I looked at every one of them. We even sat in them and dreamed about what it would be like to have one of our own. I had my favorite girlfriend Tina with me that day. She encouraged me "Molly you should splurge. You and the kids deserve all the happiness. Plus, you can afford it." The kids and I agreed on our favorite hot tub with the cedar house built around it that had a window on the top so you could gaze out at the stars.

The total for all of that, including delivery and set-up, was just over eight grand. Tina and I came back the next day with my bank bag and I counted out the cash to the salesperson. I was on top of the world. I felt like Napoleon at long last. I had arrived. A few days later, they installed the hot tub. It was so big, and the kids were so little that they used it like a swimming pool. We were living a dream.

As Christmas approached, I purchased numerous gifts for them. Things they asked for and things they hadn't even thought of. Other people bought them gifts as well, including their grandparents and most of my friends. After about an hour and a half in, they were getting grumpy. They weren't even halfway through opening their presents. I couldn't understand. I thought they were being ungrateful. As it turned out, they really just wanted to play with the ones they had already opened.

I learned several valuable lessons that year. First, my kids needed mom, not just what I could buy them. Second, I was clearly trying to overcompensate for the loss of their parents no longer being together. And lastly, sometimes less is more.

Chapter Ten
"The Beginning of the End"

Everything in life was going so well for us. The kids and I were going to a little local church on Sunday. We had a family of friends who not only cared about us but also cared for us. Tina and I spent lots of time together; she practically lived with us. My kids loved my close friends, and they were very happy and just a little spoiled.

If McDonald's or Burger King came out with a new toy or movie gimmick, the kids had to have it. If we went through the drive-through and it wasn't the one they needed to complete the set, my son would have a total meltdown. But other than stuff like that, they were doing quite well. Rose had good grades. Adam struggled in kindergarten. Ever since the incident of abuse with his father, Adam has had trouble sleeping. Unfortunately, he was forced to repeat kindergarten.

Soon after we installed the hot tub, my cousin Brandon called me. He rang the farm in New York, and asked dad for my number. Apparently, he was a part of a touring team of male strippers. I hadn't seen or spoken to him since high school. He told me that he would be passing through Oklahoma, and if he could stop by.

Tina and I were getting all dressed up as we were heading out to a music concert. There was a knock at the door. I opened it. It was my cousin, who was accompanied by a friend. He introduced me to his buddy (I must stop here to describe to the reader that this man had the exact body as Channing Tantum in the movie Magic

Mike). I could not take my eyes off him. The two of us could not take our eyes off each other.

My cousin introduced me to his boss, Donnie. He said, "We live in Tampa but travel all over the country doing shows". This fine specimen of a man was covered in tattoos and had just been released from prison for the third time, and I had one dominating thought which was, "I can save him!" I believed I could fix this man. I think that when Donnie looked at me and my surroundings, he likely had similar thoughts.

We were like magnets. The attraction was beyond physical. I could look into his eyes and see his soul. What I saw and heard was a lifetime of pain and heartache. We trauma-bonded for sure. (trauma bonding is an unhealthy emotional attachment shared by victims of manipulation and abuse).

They were supposed to stay a night or two, but that turned into a week. Donnie was extremely attentive and affectionate. He was passionate about exercise. We would lift weights during the day, lay in the hot tub, and cuddle at night.

It was clear to me that my cousin had a drug problem. He didn't even know anyone in that town but would be gone for days. When he returned to my house, he slept like he was in a coma. He barely ate any food. There were a couple of times that Donnie rolled a joint, but I didn't smoke. I did not find it particularly distressing since many of my acquaintances smoked marijuana as well. I thought nothing of it.

When the week was over, and the rest of the crew had enough and wanted to leave, he finally submitted to the team, and they pulled out to return to Tampa. These were four grown men in a car traveling for weeks at a time, and they wanted to go home to their own lives and girlfriends.

Before they left, he lifted me up in his arms and asked me, "Will you be my girl?" This should have been a red flag, but I completely ignored it. I was smitten. This man desired me despite his only possession being a black trash bag containing filthy clothes. I said yes, of course.

I had no idea at the time, but this was the beginning of the end. Life as I knew it was about to be over. What would my life have been like had I just said no? How would the lives of my children turn out if I had walked away right then? I stay awake some nights to this day, wishing I could go back to that moment and choose differently.

Chapter Eleven
"Tattoos and an Heirloom Ring"

Dating across the country was very exciting. Donnie and I had a whirlwind romance. Because I still lived in Oklahoma and he lived in Florida, I only saw what he wanted me to see. He was very much an actor.

My favorite city was Las Vegas; he favored New Orleans. Even though he was also an adult entertainer, he barely made enough money to cover his gym membership and protein to stay as muscular as he was all the time.

I paid for all the plane tickets, hotels, and expensive restaurants. I mostly used my credit cards because at the time he would tell me that when he got his money right, he would pay me back half of everything. I wanted to believe him.

When we were apart, he would call me about 10 times a day. I understand that this should have been a warning sign, but at that moment, I was amazed by his intense love and obsession with me.

I bought myself an AT&T cell phone in 1996 when they were still new. It was very expensive, and back then you paid for every minute. My cell phone bill each month would be between $800and one thousand dollars. If I didn't answer each call, then he would freak out and accuse me of cheating.

When I did answer the phone, he would have me yell into the air around me: "If you are with me right now, you're a fool because I belong to Donnie T." Once I complied, he would calm down and feel more comfortable. I should have been scared; instead, I felt great compassion for him.

Donnie had lived a life of betrayal. Every woman he had ever loved had wronged him, including his mother. He would tell me stories of catching females in the act of cheating. He frequently recounted how his mother had called his parole officer years ago, causing him to be violated and sent back to prison. He was deeply damaged. However, I was as well.

In October of 1996, I arrived in New Orleans for the first time. Donnie and his crew were there dancing on Bourbon Street and had several gigs to do. He had been suggesting to me that if I truly were his, I should have his name tattooed on me. He was more than willing to get my name permanently inked onto him.

On our first full day there, we went out to restaurants, followed by shopping. We went into this beautiful antique store. There was this stunning platinum diamond heirloom engagement ring. I loved it. Donnie said that I should have it. He had zero credit, but if I put it on my credit card, then he could make the monthly payments until it was paid off. I could picture my life with him. He hadn't physically hurt me at all since I met him. I said yes.

That evening he got on one knee and proposed to me with the antique ring. I felt so special and loved by him. He had a way of making me feel like I was the only woman in the world, and he would die if he couldn't have me. I wanted to love him and heal him. I had no intention of ever cheating on him, so his extreme jealousy was just fine with me.

It wasn't enough for us to just be engaged. Right away, he started pushing the topic of tattoos. His reasoning was that a ring could be slipped off the finger. If I really was fully committed, then what could it hurt, to put his name on me permanently? Especially if the tattoo was somewhere only, he could see it?

That is exactly how he talked me into it. He started to question my devotion to him. The second day of our trip to New Orleans was spent looking for a place to get ink done. Donnie went first. He got my name in cursive, in very large writing, on his right bicep muscle. Now it was my turn. That is when he explained to the artist and me where he wanted his name tattooed. I allowed them to ink his name in small letters on a very private part of my female anatomy.

What was I thinking? That's what went through my mind as we walked back to the hotel that night. Donnie was smiling from ear to ear and shouting into the streets of New Orleans "You know it's yours when it's got your name on it!" The only comfort I had that night was knowing that I had shown him, in the ultimate way, that I was his. Perhaps he could now finally relax and cease demanding me to demonstrate that I was not like these other women.

Chapter Twelve
"The Cracks of the Mask"

After returning to Oklahoma, I missed him. He would call me incessantly, so I knew he missed me too. I invited Donnie to take some time off work and stay with me and the kids for a while.

I enjoyed this period. We were "playing house." We would go lift weights and exercise. We ate lots of great food. I had my friends over often. I was trying to get him to see that family life had its appeal.

There were a couple of times that I had to drive him around or ask my friends to see who knew where to get marijuana. I wasn't into it but knew that some of my friends smoked, so it really didn't bother me all that much.

I would pray during our meals and even before bedtime. I could tell that this was something that he wasn't used to being around, but he never objected. He would talk about his friends back in Florida and the exciting fast life that he missed.

I was more focused on getting things like his eyes checked out. Donnie could hardly see and had been without glasses for years. He had neglected things like teeth, hearing, and vision. With my help, we got him back on track and healthy. I bought him a pair of eyeglasses. This was the first pair of decent glasses he had owned in years. He wore those thick Coke bottle glasses. I wondered how in the world he survived before I came along. I bought him more weights for our gym in the garage. He received all the new gear, including nice shoes and clothes. I tried desperately to make him happy. It appeared to be working.

I remember this one time that a friend of his from Florida was passing through. I came home from work, and they were both completely intoxicated. I found a small bottle of clear liquid that stunk so badly. I had no idea what it was. When I asked about it, he explained that it was GHB. Bodybuilders commonly used this street drug, also known as a date rape drug, to achieve deep REM sleep. But of course, there were many people that abused it.

There was an evening when Donnie was using my car to run an errand. Tina and I were at the house alone with his friend. This guy was clearly out of control, persistently attempting to touch us and making inappropriate comments to both of us. He was truly out of his mind.

Knowing how jealous and possessive Donnie was, Tina and I hid in my room and locked the door. About an hour later, Donnie came pounding on the door with all his weight, demanding that we open it. I was genuinely terrified. I think we both thought this was exactly what he would have wanted us to do in that situation, but we were wrong.

I pulled the door open, and he came rushing in. There was rage in his eyes. I quickly explained how the evening played out and all about his friend's behavior. He guided me into the living room, revealing his buddy's unconscious state on the couch, before accusing me of having sex with my girlfriend during his absence. I was humiliated.

I just laughed at him. I did not intend to do so, but was he insane? Did he think I made up that whole story so I could sneak some extra sex in? Did he think that I was a total pig, that cheats the moment my lover is momentarily away? What kind of person did he think I was?

Quickly I remembered how damaged and betrayed he had been. All those stories he had told me about being cheated on which we had in common. I still could remember how that felt. I settled down and quickly turned into a compassionate caregiver again. I slowly explained the situation and asked him politely what he would have preferred me to do next time.

I was the one that apologized to him. I tried to put myself in his shoes and see it from his perspective. I think that's what I always ended up doing in my relationships. I would sacrifice my own dignity. I would replace my needs with theirs. I would immerse myself completely to prevent another individual from succumbing to emotional pain. Donnie had me right where he wanted me.

News began to spread in my small friend group. The tattoo, the extremely possessive behavior, and the incessant phone calls were all contributing factors. The people who loved me were all seeing through the cracks of the mask that he wore, but I just wouldn't hear it. They all tried desperately to warn me. I just couldn't walk away. I didn't want to be another person who hurt him or abandoned him. He was mine, and I was going to save him.

Chapter Thirteen
"Barbie and Ken"

If you count from the day we met until the day we were married, it would add up to three months. Our brief courtship took place across the country. Donnie continued to live most of that time in Tampa; the kids and I were in Oklahoma.

We were set to be married on New Year's Eve in Las Vegas. I had asked my dearest friend Tina to stand with me and be my maid of honor. She said yes, but only after rigorously trying to talk me out of it. His friends were all as broke as he was. He had made one friend while staying at my house, and since that friend was dating Tina, it made sense for him to ask her boyfriend to be his best man.

I remember getting fitted for this beautiful wedding dress. I recall all the dreams that I had for our life together. If anyone had told me that the dream would turn into the nightmare that it did, I probably wouldn't have believed it.

We invited my parents (it was their wedding anniversary) and they flew out to Vegas to meet us. We spent as much time with them as we could while we were there. Donnie was just as charming as ever. I could tell my mom really liked him. She lit up every time he smiled. He was very likable.

We played slots, went to the shows, went shopping, and went out to the nicest restaurants. Donnie was the biggest Elvis Presley fan I had ever known, and I knew of many. I went to several of his shows, and most of his performances were based on Presley. He did a very sexy routine to "Jailhouse Rock" among others.

He often expressed his aspiration to lead a life akin to that of Elvis Presley, but regrettably, he would also meet his demise in the same manner. It only made sense that we would get married in one of those little chapels on the strip in Las Vegas. On the day of the wedding, my dad attempted to talk him out of it, a fact I didn't discover until later. But it just wasn't to be. There was something magnetizing between the two of us; I used to think it was fate, now I believe it was brokenness.

We faced each other. We both promised to love, honor, and cherish each other. In sickness and in health. For better or for worse. In the good times and the bad. Forsaking all others. This was the pledge I made. And I meant every word of it. I had no idea that just one year, five months, and 17 days later it would all end. Is it better to have loved and lost than never to have loved at all?

We strolled around Vegas that night in our wedding attire. So many people were calling out to us, even taking our pictures. He was a tall, chiseled handsome man, while I was a busty blonde with a tiny waist. Strangers were calling us "Barbie and Ken." It really was a magical night.

Still right underneath the surface of his smile was this seething jealousy. If I even looked at someone for more than a second, he would stare down and glare at me. I should have run. I just couldn't see all the signs that were there.

I had been in a marriage with a man that barely acknowledged me. This new relationship felt like such an upgrade at the time. Nothing could have prepared me for what was to come.

Chapter Fourteen
"Like Father Like Son"

We returned home to Oklahoma as a married couple. Donnie was going stir crazy. I don't think the quiet, simple life was for him. He constantly talked about Tampa and the friends and lifestyle he sorely missed.

He was not a fan of Jimmy at all. Even though he was aware of the abuse and horrors I had endured, he continued to act as if this man was a rival or a threat to his pride. I had stored some of Jimmy's things in my garage because they didn't fit into his tiny apartment. He had a large box, the size of a refrigerator, filled with his nicer clothes.

Shortly after the attempted rape, I had purchased a 9mm handgun. One day I heard the gun go off several times in a row. I came running out into the garage, and there he was. Donnie was beaming, aiming the gun at the clothing box. He had put several holes in Jimmy's best clothes.

I was shocked. I tried to ask what he was thinking. Why would he do something like that to another man's property? It made no sense to me whatsoever. This line of questioning only fueled his anger, so I just let it go. I took the firearm away and locked it in the safe.

When we did pickups or drop-offs with the kids, Donnie would always make sure he pumped the weights first. He would jump out of the car with no shirt on and flex all his muscles. It was almost like he loved to intimidate people. Especially other men. To top it off, he would always make these big public displays of affection, just to rub it in his face.

One night, while we were sound asleep, the house phone rang. Donnie jumped up and answered it and then shook me awake. It was Jimmy's mom calling all the way from New York. I knew it could only be bad news; she was never fond of me. She asked me to go in person and tell her son what had happened.

If I had to guess, the way that Jimmy abused me was observed behavior. James, his father, had recently experienced the departure of his second wife, who had taken their young son and seemingly moved on with her life. I had heard stories of the abuse she had suffered. I totally understood why she left, better than anyone.

Apparently, she had only moved one town over. She had been dating a younger man, but only casually for a few months. James was a longtime hunter. He crawled through parts of the woods on his stomach, carrying his rifle. He spotted the new guy out in the garage, with his back turned toward the trees. James fired his rifle several times. Shooting and killing the unarmed man in the back. Soon after, when the police were closing in on him, he somehow managed to turn the rifle around and shot himself. He took his own life.

This was my worst nightmare. This was the threat that had been made to me many times over the years by his son. It was the exact type of scenario that haunted my dreams. The only difference was that I consistently believed I would die first.

I went to deliver the news to my ex-husband. His father was his hero and could do nothing wrong in his eyes. He was overcome with grief. In the very next breath, he told me, "That's exactly what I should do to you!"

I was already frightened of living so close to him, but after this event, my fear went to the next level. When Donnie suggested a trip to Florida, I quickly agreed. I couldn't get out of that state fast enough.

Chapter Fifteen
"Techno Music and Ecstasy"

We booked our trip to Tampa. I had only ever been to Plantation, Florida. My sweet Aunt Karen, who was my biological father's older sister, invited me when I was 13 years old. My mom had been complaining to her that I was "boy crazy." If you consider liking a particular boy to be crazy, then yes, I certainly was.

I spent a week there with my aunt and her husband and kids. They had always lived out of state, but anytime they were in New York, they would come to visit my mother and me. I was truly grateful because, without her and one of her other sisters, I would have been completely disconnected from my father. It was on that trip as a young teenage girl that I had begun a personal relationship with God that would carry me through my lifetime.

I was excited to get out of Oklahoma and away from potential danger. My dear friend Tina was more like family than a friend to me. She had always wanted to go see the sunshine state. So, when she begged Donnie, he reluctantly agreed to let her come on our trip with us.

Dwayne was the first acquaintance of his we encountered. He lived in a small one-bedroom apartment that was just a short walk from St. Pete Beach. He was quite a few years older than Donnie and they had spent many years in prison together. The guy was strange but kind. When he would excuse himself and lock himself in his bedroom, Donnie would explain to me that he had a problem with smoking crack cocaine. I was 27 years old and had never been exposed to hard drugs.

Even though I had been an adult entertainer for years, I was quite the square. Other than the occasional glass of wine or mixed drink, I was a completely sober person. I had never even been drunk while dancing. The point of my being at work was to make money to support my kids. I never received a single dollar of child support, not ever. I knew other dancers who smoked weed. I even heard rumors of some that did "coke," but it was totally frowned upon where I was working. I had never even heard of crack cocaine.

Later that day, Donnie asked me to take him in the rental car to the mall. Apparently, he owed somebody money. He said it was important that he pay this guy back or he would never be safe in Florida again. I guess I didn't want to know the answer, because I never asked the question of why.

As we were pulling up to West Shore Mall, he told me he was $300 short and asked if he could borrow the money if he paid me back. By now, his words had instilled in me a sense of fear for his safety, so naturally, I agreed and handed over the cash. Here we were in the parking lot of a Florida mall on vacation and my thought was "It's time to go shop." I was getting ready to step out of the car, but he stopped me and stated he did not want me to get out. I ended up staying in the car while he disappeared. He was gone for a while. Just when I was starting to panic, he returned to the car, unharmed. "Let's go," he said.

That night we were going clubbing in Ybor City. I had never been, but I had learned all sorts of cool things about this town. One thing I heard was that they close some of the streets at night to cars. It's a place where you can walk from clubs to restaurants without any traffic. There were police officers everywhere, which made me feel very safe.

As soon as we arrived at the club, we met up with a group of Donnie's friends. These guys were all muscular and attractive too. One of them put something into the palm of his hand. Soon after, he took Tina and me aside. He said, "Look, I have these three pills; they are called ecstasy. Do you girls want to try some?" Tina, being more experienced than me, eagerly embraced the opportunity to try something new. I was more hesitant.

It took some persuasion. Not just from Donnie, but also from Tina. They told me I would be safe, and nothing bad would happen. He assured me that they are not addictive and that you will likely find them enjoyable. I didn't want to be the man out, so I reluctantly agreed to try, but only a half of one.

This was my first encounter with drugs. Yes, I had smoked a joint at a graduation party at the end of my senior year of high school, but I hated it and never did it again. I wish I could say that this night was terrible and that I didn't enjoy myself, but that wouldn't be true.

Suddenly the lights were magical and transformative. I could feel the music. If a person brushed against my arm, it felt like they touched my soul. There was a connection. I felt for the first time like I was safe. I felt beautiful and whole. I wanted to touch, kiss, and hold every person that I saw with my eyes.

The story I was told later was that I went into the ladies' room at the club and didn't want to come out. I was posted up there for close to an hour. He had to send Tina in to get me. Apparently, I was in there telling each woman how stunning she was. I was complimenting their hair, eyes, teeth, and clothes. I was spreading cheer and uplifting women. It felt like we were all connected. I felt amazing.

I danced to every single song. I could not sit down. I was drenched in sweat. I had never heard techno music before, but now it was a part of me. And I was a part of it. At least that's how it felt when I was on that drug.

After that club closed, we headed to Fantasy Ranch, an after-hours club. I was dancing closely with this sexy blonde lady. Surprisingly, Donnie wasn't jealous or angry. I think he thought it was cute that I was so smitten with the pretty girls. But it was more than that. It was the black lights and the feel of the techno music in my body. I wasn't trying to be gay; I was just enjoying the beauty of everything around me.

On the negative side, I experienced the most severe case of cottonmouth in my life. I struggled very hard to fall asleep. It was late the next afternoon, with the sun glaring, when I finally managed to close my eyes. It was fun, but I was glad that the trip was finally over.

Chapter Sixteen
"Pennies on the Dollars"

On the last day we spent in Tampa, we used our time to tour houses and make phone calls. I hadn't made a commitment to move yet, however, I didn't need convincing arguments to justify leaving Oklahoma and my ex-husband behind. I had established my own family there, but ever since his father's death, I was constantly on high alert, fearing for my life.

On our way to the airport, we stopped in Carrollwood and checked out a 4-bedroom house with a swimming pool. The house also featured an office that could serve as an additional bedroom. Even though the house was smaller and not as nice as the stunning home we already lived in, it did have a pool. I knew the kids would love it, so I put in an offer on the house, and we flew back home.

Soon after I returned to Oklahoma, they accepted my offer. Now I have a decision to make. Should I sell the home and downsize? Should I uproot the kids from the only life they have known? Should I move them over a thousand miles away from their father? This was not an easy decision.

I sat down and discussed it with my renter. My stripper friend who was renting our original house in Del City was making a lot more money at work and she had her eye on my new house in Moore. She stayed and watched our house for us while we were out of town. She was determined that she could now afford the additional money. The timing was great because Jimmy's apartment lease was up. He was able to afford the mortgage for our first home where currently my coworker had been renting. I couldn't buy the third home if the other two were still in my name.

To qualify for another home loan, I needed to let Jimmy have the first home. I needed a large cash down payment, so I set up a "lease to own" contract with my friend, the adult entertainer. I had been making additional mortgage payments since I had bought that house. I was able to charge her more than what I owed for the monthly payments. She gave me a large cash down payment, which I then used to purchase my third home in Florida. Now everyone was happy, including my kid's father. I was proud of myself. How many adults had purchased their third home at the age of 27? I felt like I was my own version of an entrepreneur.

Unfortunately, the new home had much smaller, normal-sized rooms. I had bought grand-sized furniture for the previous house because regular furniture looked too small in it. I had to list all the luxury furniture I had spent months working and saving for in the newspaper. Even worse, most people who fell in love with the furniture were unable to pay what it was worth. They just couldn't afford it, and I was running out of time. I ended up having to sell it all for pennies on the dollar.

The kids were sad, too. They previously had an entire upstairs to themselves. They had more toys than any kids I had ever met. We even had a cinnamon capuchin monkey that I had bought the kids as an exotic pet. His name was Rowdy; and the name suited him very well. He was a very talented pickpocket. We found his stashes all over the house when we packed up to move. We found watches, lighters, and coins.

I had always been obsessed with monkeys. Back then, in Oklahoma, it wasn't illegal to own one. A regular customer of mine from the club had bought him for me; later, when we got into an argument, I paid him back. I didn't want to owe this guy anything.

This kind of monkey has a long life span and is considered an adult at the age of three. Rowdy was close to that age already. If I was going to rehome him, I needed to do it soon. Thankfully, my favorite DJ at the club developed an obsession with him. He was newly married, and they had a home in the country with several acres of land. The choice was obvious. This monkey was part of the family. He deserved to be with someone who would love and care for him. My friend later reported to me that his dog and the monkey became the best of friends.

The D.J. was unable to repay the thousands of dollars I had paid for him, so I asked him to reimburse the cost of all the custom-built cages we had constructed for him. This way I could recuperate some of my financial losses.

The sale of the cages, the furniture, and the down payment on the house was put in the bank. I wasn't sure what I would do for work once I got there, so I thought the cushion would help us get started.

A couple of good friends from Oklahoma drove a U-Haul truck, and Donnie and I loaded up the two cars with the kids and some of our valuables. We said our goodbyes to Oklahoma. It was a sad day. One chapter was closing, but a brand new one was about to open.

Chapter Seventeen
"Cannon Ball"

The kids were beyond happy once we arrived in Florida and got settled into our new home. The very first thing they did was shed their clothes and jump straight into the pool. My little boy yelled "Cannonball" as he plunged into the water.

Each kid got to pick their own room. My son Adam had a bunk bed set. My daughter Rose was barely able to squeeze her queen-sized bedroom set in her room. She had everything unpacked and organized all by herself. She was always very mature for her age. I think because I was only a child when I had her, I talked to her more like she was a best friend than a child. Now I regret how quickly she had to grow up.

At first, everything was perfectly normal. We had a large weight set (which Donnie kept adding too) in our dining area. Regardless of the weather, his health, or fatigue, he consistently used the weights. It amazed me how committed he was to his body and physical strength. He explained to me that he was so skinny growing up that he was teased all the time. Even his little sister Vickie had called him "Olive Oil"; after the wife of Popeye the sailor man. Had it not been for my income and credit cards, I'm uncertain how he would have managed to eat the copious amounts of food he consumed to maintain his size.

Donnie was always spending money in the nutrition shops on supplements and whey protein powders. He had such a naturally fast metabolism, so he burned up everything he put in his mouth. And boy did he eat a lot.

This period, when we initially arrived in Florida, was characterized by many positive aspects. There wasn't any fighting or arguing, probably because I didn't know anyone and rarely left the house. I felt like maybe I had made the best decision after all. He was finally happy and even seemed to feel secure for the first time. You know the saying "If momma ain't happy, ain't nobody happy?" Well, that was true, but not for me, for Donnie.

I didn't work during this time. I stayed home, did laundry, cooked meals, cared for the kids, and cleaned. It was peaceful and very fulfilling. Donnie was still doing his male stripper gigs a couple of times per week. He ended up taking my cell phone for himself. Which made sense because I was always home, and we had a landline.

When we left Oklahoma, I owned a brand-new Mazda 626, which was the first new car I ever had. That car was my baby she even had a name. I worked hard to have nice things. I also had a used white Toyota Corolla. Normally, I wouldn't allow anyone to drive my car, so he ended up driving the Corolla. However, Donnie didn't like it. That car was not up to his standards.

He kept complaining and putting pressure on me. The only good point that he made was that he had no credit. I couldn't put him on the mortgage, which he really wanted, because the bank wouldn't have loaned us the money. Therefore, we decided to go car shopping together.

This is a man who had nothing when I met him. He would couch surf with his friends; he went from friend to friend and crashed a couple of nights on their couches. His only possessions fit in a large black trash bag. However, the paid-off Corolla did not meet his expectations.

There were several good values on the dealer's lot. Donnie did not like any of them. He had his eyes set on a barely used black Toyota 4-Runner. Even with the trade-in of my other car, the payments were $670 per month. It was ridiculous. My payment for my new Mazda was almost half that. Did I say no? Of course not. I sat there and submitted whatever he wanted. I knew deep down that I would be the one who had to make the payments. I cosigned, and he drove that SUV out of the parking lot.

While driving that 4-runner, he was truly in his element. Donnie grew up poor. He had spent many of his adult years in prison. Now he had this sick whip. He was full of himself. He stopped coming home directly after his shows. I would call sometimes, and he wouldn't answer for hours. Despite his intense jealousy, I didn't consider myself suspicious.

He accidentally left the cell phone at home one night when he was running late. I heard it ringing. I went and located the phone and answered it, thinking it was probably one of his buddies checking to see when he would get to the show. I was wrong. A woman answered when I said hello. "Who is this?" I calmly asked. She asked for Donnie. I said, "he isn't here. Who is this?" She said, "if your husband is a real man, then ask him. He will tell you who I am." Then she hung up the phone.

When he returned that night, I told him what happened. When I told him her exact words, he told me the truth. It was his ex-stripper girlfriend who broke his heart. The one he had caught cheating on him. Then he admitted to me that they were sleeping together and that it was my fault. In his mind, I hadn't become the ideal wife he had expected. I was blown away.

I should have run as fast and as far as I could get. This man was a psycho over me. He would put me through the craziest tests. He would check me closely and even smell between my legs when

I came home from work prior to this. He had held a sharp knife against my skin many times and threatened to cut off my lady parts if I ever cheated on him. I always had to keep proving myself. I swear on everything, I had never considered cheating on him.

He had me so brainwashed that even though I was hurt and devastated, I stayed. My thinking was that it hadn't been enough time. He was so traumatized from his past relationships that I was just going to have to double down so he would know that I was the one woman that he could trust. I had no interest in any other man. I was committed.

Chapter Eighteen
"Throwing Rocks from a Glass House"

During these months of getting to know my groom, he would tell me these nightmarish stories. He only had one sibling; a younger sister named Vickie. They had been raised in Wisconsin. As soon as Donnie reached adulthood, he made every effort to distance himself from his mother. That's how he ended up in Tampa.

Donnie told me stories of how his and Vickie's mom, Sharon, had interfered. In addition to reporting her son for possessing a handgun during his parole period, which resulted in his return to prison; she also filed reports against her own daughter with the Department of Children and Families.

According to my husband, his mother was no angel herself. She was the person living in the glass house, throwing rocks at others. Sharon was addicted to prescription drugs. She even had a procedure that involved placing a morphine pump under her skin, specifically in the stomach area, and had it refilled every month.

Vickie was a single mom, still living in rural Wisconsin where they grew up. She had recently given birth to her second son. When she gave birth to her first son as a teenager, he was widely perceived as a difficult child. My husband stated that the nephew was now a teenager and had already faced expulsion from school.

My husband was so excited. It had been a decade since he had seen his sister. She had invited us to her wedding in Racine, Wisconsin. She was to marry the father of her second child.

We had already made a commitment and arrangements before the phone call incident I had with his ex-girlfriend. Donnie swore that he deeply regretted cheating and that he had broken off the relationship. Even though I had been shocked and hurt, I had already forgiven him.

We packed up the kids and our suitcase, and we hit the road. It was quite a long ride from Tampa to Racine, and unbeknownst to me, Donnie had brought a bottle of that GHB with him. He loved the effects of that drug.

The kids were singing songs. We were scouting the other vehicles for different state license tags. All things considered; it was a fun trip. He took us to his mom's place in Wisconsin, where we could settle in for a few days. There was room for the four of us to stay.

I could tell his mom had missed him. Sharon reacted as if a famous person had arrived. She and I spoke privately on several occasions about her desire to be a part of his life again. Donnie kept her at arm's length. He was detached and cold around her.

After the wedding and before we returned to Tampa, she asked him if she and her boyfriend could move to Florida to be a part of his life. To be a family again? He told her "You know what mom; I don't care what you do."

Shortly after that trip, she showed up. She had leased an apartment in Clearwater. They had filled a U-Haul truck and station wagon with their belongings. Donnie and I drove over one day so he could help them unload the truck. I was trying to make peace between them. I felt bad for her. I tried putting myself in her shoes. It was to appease me that he went there that day to help her.

Chapter Nineteen
"Not Around the Kids"

While we were in Wisconsin for the wedding, Donnie let my cousin and his girlfriend move into one of the bedrooms of our house. It made sense at the time. I hadn't started working yet, and each dollar he earned from stripping vanished in less than a day, leaving me with no money to pay the bills.

It was clearly time for me to return to work. I never considered myself better than anyone else. However, the adult entertainment industry in Florida differed significantly from my previous experiences. Most of the clubs in Tampa are fully nude. I was very troubled by this.

Thankfully someone told me about a gentleman's club on the causeway called "Scarlett's". I had to get on stage and audition. I was hired immediately. This was not a nude club; it was strictly topless. They also sold alcohol there. I was hoping it would be as lucrative as my previous establishment. Sadly, that was not to be.

With so many strip joints saturating the area, competition was fierce. Most customers likely felt that they received better value for their money at the full-nude friction clubs. I had to work twice as many shifts, twice as many hours, and for only half the pay I was used to making. But it was a job, and we needed the money.

I would often speak to Donnie about getting a real job. Perhaps a 9-to-5 position during the week would suffice. I begged him to please contribute something to the household expenses. He would say "I'm a convicted felon, I have no skills and have spent most of my adult life in jail or prison." No matter what the excuses were, it was a huge burden for me. Not only was I solely responsible for supporting my children, but I had also been providing for him financially since the day we first met. It was getting exhausting.

Thankfully, my cousin's girlfriend also worked as a stripper. She was able to pitch in on rent and even food from time to time. They mostly spent their time locked in their bedroom doing drugs. I shouldn't have allowed people like that in my home, but my own husband seemed to have the same problems himself. My rule was "not around the kids."

I was barely keeping up with the bills, and I made a friend at the club. I needed someone to care for me and have my back. She was making decent money but was wasting it staying in hotels all the time. She had no credit history and asked if she could also rent a room. Her name was Christie, and I said yes. After all, we had a space that was perfectly suited for conversion into a bedroom. No one was using that area anyway.

During this time my husband became obsessed with his size. He was tall, muscular, and lean. Any woman would have traded husbands with me, as far as his looks went anyway. Every friend I had was jealous and told me how lucky I was.

His dancing buddies introduced him to steroids. I was not happy about this at all. Donnie seemed to have all this information about the benefits and tried to convince me that nothing bad would happen. He promised to be careful with them.

He was never happy with his progress in lifting weights. He believed that his body played a crucial role in the quality of his life, and this held tremendous importance. Unfortunately, the steroids he was taking necessitated needle injections. This required that he be able to turn his torso clockwise while lifting his arm in the air and pushing this large needle into the muscle. He was so "jacked" already that he couldn't physically do it to himself.

I didn't have a choice. There was no option to deny him. It wasn't a request. He instructed me on how to give him these shots. Not only did he constantly examine my body whenever we were apart, searching for signs of another man, but there were also constant threats. These were very detailed and well-thought-out threats of physical harm. He had already begun smacking me around. I was like a robot, completely numb inside. I felt like a mannequin, there for his pleasure only.

Chapter Twenty
"Doubled Down"

Every day of our relationship wasn't bad. There were some good days. I remember we would go to Blockbuster Video and rent a whole pile of movies. The whole family, including our friends, would spend hours in front of the television. Both Donnie and little Adam were great at doing character impersonations. They were very entertaining. We placed so many Papa John's orders that the delivery drivers knew us by our first names.

My husband was very affectionate. Sometimes he would act like a real knight in shining armor when listening to my girlfriend's problems. He could be compassionate and even thoughtful at times. He would even bring me single roses and teddy bears when returning from his gigs.

Other than the severe mental torture, the main problem was his substance use. I wasn't raised in a home with drugs or excessive alcohol consumption. Even when I lived in Oklahoma, I maintained a relatively sheltered lifestyle. The only drug I was familiar with was marijuana.

If Donnie was awake and his eyes were open, he was searching for something to alter his mind. I would catch him swallowing a handful of pills and ask, "What was that?" He would laugh and say, "I took one blue pill, and two green ones."

I don't know if he even knew what he was taking half the time. He smoked weed every day. He drank alcohol almost every day as well.

I remember clearly calling my stepfather. He was someone that I trusted, much more worldly than I was. I said "Dad, I don't know what to do. Donnie is a drug addict." I was genuinely surprised. I was aware of the marijuana (which didn't bother me; I knew plenty of people who smoked), but that was all I knew prior to moving to Tampa. Donnie only let me see what he wanted me to see. He was very much an actor, wearing a mask all the time. My father said to me, "Molly, your husband is a grown-ass man. You will never change him. From my perspective, you have two options to consider. First, you could sell your house, bring the kids and move back to New York. Let Mom and I help you." This was not an option for me. I already knew that N.Y. was a non-starter. "Or you can stay and try to make your marriage work. But you will never change him."

I really considered my father's words. I contemplated all the experiences I had leading up to this moment. I made all the sacrifices necessary. I was invested in this relationship. This was my second marriage. I've always been an overachiever. Failing was not an option for me. I was determined to turn this thing around. I set out to fix this man, and I had failed. I should have run for my life. Instead, I doubled down.

At first, I decided to just go with the flow. I decided to stop pushing him in this direction. If he desired to indulge and get loaded, I stopped my criticism and picked my battles. I figured if I stopped "nagging", as he would call it, then maybe it would not be as much fun to him. I thought I just needed to stop challenging him so much.

That didn't last long. Once he knew he had free reign, he was off to the races. My daughter would be accompanied by her little friend, while Donnie would be unconscious, lying on the floor, appearing near lifeless. Rose would cautiously step over him and pull her friend along. I once heard her say "Don't worry, that's my stepdad. He does this all the time."

When that didn't work, I couldn't help but think what was the big deal? I often wondered what he loved so much about it. I just couldn't see it after watching him all the time. That is when my mantra changed to If you can't beat him, then maybe, join him.

I wouldn't do as much as him, but whatever he was doing for that day, I would try it. Sometimes it was GHB, or ecstasy. Other times it was pills. The only drug he forbade me to try was cocaine. He knew women who were so addicted to Coke that they were willing to sell their own children for another hit.

I can't say that it was all horrible. If it were, people would never get addicted. In the beginning, it was fun. We would party during the weekends. It would be special. It was something I looked forward to. However, it quickly became unmanageable. I was baffled. I had no idea what to do. We had never heard of Narcotics Anonymous or alcoholics anonymous. Donnie's favorite t-shirt was "REHAB IS FOR QUITTERS.'

Chapter Twenty-One
"Comfortably Numb"

The club I worked at was about to undergo demolition. They were getting prepared to widen the Courtney Campbell Causeway. My housemate Christie and I were becoming very dear friends. I would have been lost without her. Especially during this time of my life.

Together we decided that of all the other local clubs, we would go dancing at the 2001 Space Odyssey. It had a room upstairs that was shaped like a spaceship. This room served as the VIP area for private one-on-one dances. This was an opportunity to earn real money, comparable to what I had been earning at Night Trips in Oklahoma City.

The steroids were making my husband extremely aggressive, even more than usual. He had bouts of depression when he wouldn't get out of bed all day. His jealousy had reached new levels too. There were nights when I would return from work, he would have me lie naked on the bed, place his knife on my genitals, and threaten to cut them off if I ever disappointed him. The other drugs he was taking weren't helping the situation either.

He had several close friends; most of them were bodybuilding male strippers. He told me stories about them getting blowjobs in the bathroom after the shows. He claimed that even those who were married cheated. When he was telling me the truth and had such disgust for his friend's behavior, I assumed he was more than likely being faithful. I never had any proof that he wasn't other than that first girl who called me on his cell phone. I didn't care for any of his friends except for Tony.

Tony was a tall, muscular man, his dirty blonde hair always falling into his face. He wasn't nearly as attractive as my husband, but his personality made up for it. He wasn't a user like some of the other guys. He was quite sweet. I could also say that he liked Christie. Donnie was well behaved when he was around; he was more respectful.

It was during this time that my cousin and his girl were kicked out. He had stolen from me a couple of times already. So, they went to live somewhere else. However, their room did not remain vacant for long. Donnie had met another couple from the club where I was working. She was a stripper named Brandy, and her boyfriend John was a vagrant who lived off her money. They had a beautiful German Sheppard dog, named Sid that instantly became part of the family. That's probably why the two of them clicked so well. They were able to send their women to work while they stayed at home and relaxed. The problem with these two was that they were on some hard-cored drugs heroin to be exact.

Donnie had been struggling greatly to detox from the GHB. Funny enough, it was the one substance that I liked the most. I had done some research, and there were in fact many health benefits to taking it, if one didn't abuse it. And to be honest, my husband convinced me that it wasn't addictive. GHB stands for gamma-hydroxybutyric acid. Bodybuilders have used this drug for years as an aesthetic and as a performance enhancer.

My husband had used so much of it that he developed a tolerance. He needed the drug to wake up in the morning. He also needed it to go to sleep at night. He had been trying to go cold turkey (which means to abruptly stop taking it) but became very ill. He was throwing up, had diarrhea, and basically couldn't eat. He was getting dehydrated but wouldn't even consider going to the hospital. His greatest concern was that someone would discover his condition, and he would end up back in jail. He made me promise to never call the paramedics or cops.

While he was trying to kick this habit, he could no longer care for the kids in the evening. I had to work as many nights per week as I could just to keep up with all the bills. On top of that, who knows how much of my money he was spending on drugs? Donnie had full access to everything. We were married for goodness' sake.

I had to pay a teenage babysitter to come sit in my home with the kids at night while I was out working. Talk about growing resentment. I didn't want outsiders in my home to start with. I legitimately worried about anyone discovering the presence of drugs in our house. My children lived in that home. I did not want to risk losing them. But my husband had become so worthless to me. He couldn't be bothered to cook dinner, give baths, check homework, or put them to bed on time. So, I had to expose myself even more. This young lady was great with my kids, and they loved all the attention. If she sat with them on the weekend, she would even take them places. I paid her a set fee in cash. I also tipped her very well. I hoped that this would help her to remember to be discreet with my business, and she was.

One night I returned home exhausted. It had been a very long and boring shift at work. I was determined to leave with the money I needed to pay the sitter and go grocery shopping. The only thing I wanted was to curl up in a ball and go to sleep. My husband was standing there in the kitchen, Pink Floyd was playing on the stereo.

He had the most peaceful look I had ever seen on his face. He was calm, cool, and relaxed. I inquired "Hey, what's going on? You look different." He looked at me like he had just seen me for the first time ever. "I feel amazing," he said. "I just tried heroin for the first time." I don't know how, but I knew deep down inside. Things were about to get worse.

Chapter Twenty-Two
"The Nightmare had Just Begun"

This was still my "go with the flow phase." I didn't know enough then about addiction or drugs to recognize how dangerous heroin was. I couldn't see that the danger had just increased exponentially. In my mind, this was just another substance. We already were using ecstasy and GHB recreationally.

We would stay up late watching movies like Pulp Fiction and Goodfellas. Most of the movies we were watching at the time portrayed substance use in a glamorous light. The other thing that made this feel more normal was that everyone that we were hanging around, without exception, was doing and using the same things we were.

We had just begun experimenting with heroin when I went for my annual OBGYN appointment and found out that I was pregnant. Now this would be my third child, but it was Donnie's first. To say that he was excited about the news would be the understatement of the year. My husband was over the moon!

He gave me baths, rubbed my belly, and talked to his child while in utero. He wasn't great at parenting with my two kids, but he for sure loved them. He was basically a giant kid himself. He liked to wake the kids up for school when he could drag himself out of bed, or if he was still up from partying all night. He would say "Rise and shine, it's butt whooping time." He chased my son all over the place, both laughing and squealing, throwing him up in the air like he was a toy.

Unfortunately, the pregnancy proved to be the most challenging period in our married life. We both needed to stop using drugs. There was no way that we could continue the way we were living. Neither of us would consider an abortion, so it was time to get clean and sober. By changing our lives, we had everything to gain and nothing to lose.

I had snorted heroin occasionally but had never injected it. I was using the same substances right along with him up until this point, but not the amounts that he was ingesting. That's why it baffled me when he couldn't stop. The more I tried to push him, the worse he seemed to get. I tried bribing him. I made threats to him. Nothing I did seemed to work. I tried reasoning with him. "Don't you want to have a healthy baby? Do you want to end up in jail and not be around to raise your child? Do you want to live?" I would ask.

I want to take a moment to explain what I have learned about addiction. There is this imaginary line that you can't see even when it's your own life. Most alcoholics or addicts don't recognize it until after they have crossed that line. If there is a satisfactory reason or motivation, then the person can either stop or moderate their consumption. However, once the individual crosses that line, the very same person becomes doomed. This person is a real alcoholic or addict. They went from being a heavy drinker, or drug user, to being the real deal. The metaphor that is commonly used is when a cucumber becomes a pickle. Once that happens, they can never go back to being a cucumber.

I hadn't crossed that line yet. I was still a moderate or recreational user. I suspect though, that my husband had crossed that line already—maybe even before he met me. His substance abuse quickly progressed from bad to awful. There were several times that he turned blue after ingesting the "substance of the day" or whatever he was taking. My roommates and myself would splash cold water on him or perform CPR. He would come out of it and then do it all over again. He was even cut off by a drug dealer. He said to Donnie, "You are the most extreme individual I have ever encountered."

By this time, the Toyota 4-Runner was now under repossession. I was tired of paying all the bills. He had never followed through with the promises to pay toward credit card payments or the payment on his truck. He was hardly ever working anyway. Why should I persist in stripping and busting my ass while pregnant? Just so I could continue to pay a babysitter to take care of the kids while my husband is THERE? No way. I was getting bitter.

He was still doing the occasional gig. At least it allowed him to leave and get out of the house. Even if there was no profit involved, I assumed it would at least be good for his ego. Plus, he couldn't go to work all strung out. Most of those times one of his buddies would come get him and bring him home. There was one night, though, when no one could. So, he asked me if he could borrow the car. However, I reminded him that this vehicle was my lifeline. He promised to be careful and come right home after the show.

The time kept ticking by, but there was no Donnie. He was not answering his phone, and he should have already returned with the car. I was starting to panic. That's when the phone rang. It was a highway patrolman. He said that my husband had fallen asleep at the wheel on the interstate coming back from work. My car drifted into the next lane and was hit by a semi-truck. Apparently, my husband was alive but incoherent. "Was he on any substances that you know of? Do you know what this bottle of clear liquid that we found in the car is?" he asked.

I had one of my roommates drive me to the hospital. I was very scared. Upon spotting him, I embraced him fiercely and clung to him tightly. Then I laid into him. "How could you do this to me? To the kids? What were you thinking?" He said "get me out of here now. Once they see that I was driving with a suspended license they might take me to jail."

He tore the I.V. out of his arm and jumped out of the gurney. I followed him out of the hospital and into the waiting car. He was panicking. I had never seen him so frightened. Thankfully, back then, the police weren't familiar with GHB. They had it in evidence but didn't quite know what it was. We took him home from the hospital. He kept apologizing to me profusely.

The very next day we went and collected my car from the "impound yard." It had to be towed to a local mechanic. It was there that I was told that I should probably just have the car totaled. I couldn't afford another car. I also couldn't go without transportation. I just had no clue where to go from here.

What has happened to my life? I thought. I just couldn't imagine how things could get any worse than they were. I was so mistaken about that. The nightmare had only just begun.

Chapter Twenty-Three
"Brass Knuckles and Unfair Fights"

This was a very challenging time of my life. As Donnie's addiction was spiraling out of control, I was seething with bitterness. I had to ask people for rides everywhere and even paid an outrageous fee for a weekly rental car once. I had no choice. They hadn't even begun the repairs on my Mazda yet. I had parent-teacher conferences, doctor appointments, grocery shopping, and work to attend to. You wouldn't know unless you were told that I was pregnant. I still maintained my figure. It was crucial to our survival that I stayed in great shape.

How long could this continue? I knew that eventually, it would become obvious that I was with a child. It made me literally sick to my stomach the way that these customers looked at and spoke to me. They didn't know that I was pregnant, but I knew. What I was doing, what I had to do, made my skin crawl.

We went to the doctor's appointment. My husband came with me for the sonogram. We both wanted to know the sex of the baby, and it was a girl. Donnie was elated! He was going to have a child of his own, a beautiful little girl.

In the same measure of excitement was his fear. He believed that the police would arrive at any moment to make an arrest. He was scared to leave the house. It was during this time that he started to share his plan with me. Donnie had this overwhelming sense of impending doom. He began to hatch a plan. He shared with me that he wanted me to take the kids, pack my things, and move back to New York with my family. He didn't want me in Florida. He desired that his daughter be born away from both him and his mother. Sharon had recently shared with him that his last name was not even that of his real father and that he was a product of molestation. Her own father sexually abused her from the age of 12 to nineteen, according to her. This information didn't bring compassion from him; instead, he hated her even more.

We did a lot of arguing that week. He was consuming more and more drugs. I was working a lot. I needed to bank as much cash as I could before I started to show. The other two ladies in the house were helping me with everything then, including feeding and getting the kids to school.

My cousin Brandon came one evening to check on me. My pearl-handled 22-pistol was lying on the headboard of my bed. He was asking how it was going with the pregnancy and the family. Throughout his entire visit, he displayed signs of extreme agitation. His eyes darted around the room while he spoke at a rapid pace. When he finally left, I glanced around and started preparing for bedtime. That's when I noticed my gun was gone.

I told Donnie what happened. He was full of rage. My cousin had developed a serious problem with crack cocaine. We had already bailed him out of trouble several times. Not only did he steal from us and pawn our valuables, but he also went missing for four days. He called me. Sounding very frightened, he said that he owed a drug dealer $400, and if we didn't pay, then they were going to kill him. Even after all that we had done, he stole from me again that night.

I could not talk my husband down this time. He was not in his right mind, and hadn't been for quite some time. He borrowed a car and left with his brass knuckles. When he returned home an hour later, he was all sweaty. He told me that he had made things right. He described to me how he had beaten the brakes off my cousin.

The very next day, his friend Tony stopped by. He wanted to talk to my husband, but I didn't want to disturb him. He was soundly sleeping and was really trying to kick his heroin habit. He was trying to do the right thing. We just let him sleep. Tony had a camcorder that was used. He told me he just needed a little cash for it. Since my own camcorder had been stolen by my cousin, and never returned, I decided to buy it.

Months later, a man I had never met approached me and inquired about the camcorder I had bought from Tony. Stupid me, I didn't have a clue that it was stolen from him and sold to me. The man's name was Bryan. He sold used cars on the corner of our streets. He was also a mutual friend with our buddy Tony. I guess once he figured it out, he confronted him, and that's how he learned that I was the one who had bought it. We hadn't even used the camera yet. I was out the cash I had paid for it, but I was going to do the right thing. I knew exactly how it felt to have people that you trusted steal from you. Bryan and I forged a friendship from there. It was a relationship that would span decades.

Chapter Twenty-Four
"A Recipe for Disaster"

My husband was very ill. He was curled up in a ball for several days sick as a dog. It seemed that the worst of the withdrawals were behind him. He got up out of bed and ate a nice, healthy breakfast. He kept it down; no more throwing up. There was a little bit of hope.

We cuddled in bed together for the first part of the day. We watched the movie "Ghost" for the first time. That was a movie with Demi Moore and Patrick Swayze. Their love was so deep that even after his murder, he continued to assist her from the afterlife. It was a very romantic story. We both loved it. Next, we watched Goodfellas again. This was Donnie's favorite movie; he knew almost every line by heart. After that, we watched Pulp Fiction for the second time ever.

The downside to having several other adults living in our home was that even if we were trying to be good and stay clean, there were drugs being used in just the other room. I discovered for myself many years later that a person is very vulnerable to relapse when they start feeling human again (after detoxing). The situation, looking back, was a recipe for disaster.

He wasn't awake long when he came out of one of their rooms claiming "They got some stuff today that is strong shit. I'm getting some. Do you want to party?" I tried to talk him out of it, but he had made up his mind. He went in and came back out with $40 worth of dope. There were other people in the house that night as well.

The young lady who was delivering the product to the house was named Amanda. She was by no means a drug dealer. It turned out she was just an addicted person who sold drugs to help pay for her high. Unbeknownst to me, she had more than just heroin on her. I didn't find out until a day later that my husband kept bugging her for Xanax bars. We all knew the danger of mixing opiates with benzos, especially him. He knew several people who had died that way.

Now that he had been using needles for a while, he had these terrible, ugly marks all over both arms. These are commonly known as track marks. Sometimes he would hit himself, sometimes John would; that's the roommate's boyfriend who injected him the first time he had tried it. But sometimes, if he was really struggling, he would tell me to do it. I was not a fan of this at all. I still had never put a needle in my own arm. But I didn't say no to him. Not about anything. Despite his dominance over me, I still loved him. I knew that if I did it there wouldn't be a bruise or a struggle, so I complied.

If you look up the definition of battered wife syndrome in the dictionary, there should be a picture of me. I was completely submissive. My husband controlled me one hundred percent. Body, mind, and spirit. I had lost all my strength. I had no fight left.

I remember it was getting dark outside. He prepared his shot and went to the bathroom to inject himself. Afterwards, he trailed me around the house while I was doing laundry and organizing the garage. I could tell that he was trashed, but no more than usual. He then drew me a bath. He got in the tub with me and was telling me to go. He wanted me to pack my suitcase, take the kids, and return to New York. It was time he told me. He then told me how much he loved me and how sorry he was for failing in so many ways. He was convinced that he had ruined my life.

After the bath, we went to bed. He was holding me closely. I was reflecting on everything he said to me that day. My heart was breaking for all that had happened. Maybe I should go to my parents' home? Maybe I should do what he wanted and leave him behind. What if he was right and he was going to be arrested soon?

That's when he started snoring loudly. I was having a hard time falling asleep that night. On top of that, I was a very light sleeper. I knew if I stayed in bed with him, it would be hours before I fell asleep. I was five months pregnant by then and had to get the kids up and ready for school early the next morning. I had never slept anywhere but in his bed since we got married, but that night I crept into my daughter's room. I had my large box fan and pillows. I climbed into bed next to her and fell asleep fast.

Chapter Twenty-Five
"A Scene from Pulp Fiction"

The next morning, we woke up a little late. I had pressed the snooze button because I was sleeping so well. I woke up next to my beautiful angel. "Get up guys we have to get dressed and ready for school," I said as I was shaking them awake. My friend and housemate Christie was already in the kitchen cooking breakfast for the kids.

We got them ready for school. They picked up their backpacks and headed for the door. I didn't want to let them bother Donnie, so we just let him sleep. I walked them to the bus stop and then returned to the house. It was a sunny, beautiful morning, not a cloud on the horizon.

When I returned to the house, Christie said there was some bacon, eggs, and toast left. My husband loved anything with protein in it. I knew he would want me to wake him up to eat. He could always go back to sleep once he finished his food. That's what I was thinking anyway.

When I walked into our bedroom, it was completely still. There was no sound at all. At first glance, it looked just like he was sleeping. But as I walked closer to him, I could see that something was very wrong. I screamed as loud as I could! I kept on screaming until all three adults ran into the room. He wasn't blue in the face like he had been previous times. This time, however, was unlike any other time. There was vomit seeping out of the side of his mouth. It also looked like something was leaking out of his ear. He was lying completely still.

We jumped into action. John and Brandy grabbed his legs and pulled him onto the floor next to the bed. I called 911 for help. I need to take a moment to acknowledge that I was breaking a significant rule. I had sworn to never call any type of officials. If you had asked me the week prior, I would promise I could have passed a lie detector test saying that I would never call outsiders into our home.

While I was on with the paramedics, I put the call on speaker phone and began performing CPR. In fact, I had already received my certification and applied lifesaving techniques multiple times in the past. I was good at it. When doing chest compressions though, each time I pressed down and let up, vomit would shoot out of his mouth. Despite the nauseating sensation, I persisted with the procedure. I had a pulse on him. It was "thready," but it was there.

The paramedics arrived shortly after. I knew what they were supposed to do, but they weren't doing it. I saw Pulp Fiction. I was honest and told them what substances he had ingested. This was before the lifesaving Narcan nasal sprays hit the market. I was expecting them to stick him in the heart with an adrenaline shot like they did in the movies.

By this point in my pregnancy, my belly was growing larger. It would have been obvious to anyone that I was pregnant. I believe they wouldn't allow me to ride in the ambulance with my husband because of that and my hostile attitude towards the team working on him. They told me which hospital they were taking him to and told me that we could meet them there.

John, Brandy's boyfriend, drove me and dropped me off at the hospital. None of them wanted to be there, especially him. After all, they had also been up all night getting high. Everyone was shocked. This wasn't like the other times he had overdone it while getting loaded.

When I arrived at the hospital and asked about my husband, a kind woman escorted me to a room that had a white door. There was a wood plaque on the door that said, "Grieving room." If I had to guess, I would say it was probably a chapel. There were pews and crosses around the room. I knew right then; no one had to tell me. My husband was gone. Was this how it ended? The vows we made to each other. The roller coaster of a nightmare we had lived, was it over? What was I going to do? All I wanted to do was reverse time and start over. Our marriage lasted for one year, five months, and 17 days. That was our entire life together. I had been robbed.

I climbed onto the gurney and held my lifeless husband in my arms for the last time. I was now a pregnant widow. Was there anything more unnatural in the world than that? Was there anything more traumatic and painful than that? Some people must bury their own children. I imagine that would be comparable to the state that I found myself in that day. I was carrying the unborn child of a man who would never see her. He would never hold her. He already loved her, and she would never get to know him.

For days I lay in our bed, curled up in a fetal position. Calling out to heaven, asking God WHY?????? Was this a punishment? Was this a nightmare? Could I please go to sleep and wake up and this not be true? My parents came to Florida right away to try and help. Even my biological father made the trip; they were all speaking to each other and getting along. Donnie's mom was in Wisconsin getting the last load of their belongings so they could start a new life in Florida. She dreamed of repairing things with her son, but it was too late.

Chapter Twenty-Six
"Someone to Blame"

The days following my husband's death were a blur. I was in a constant state of denial. It would take me a few minutes after I awoke from sleep to remember that he was gone. When I was successful at getting quality rest, he would meet me in my dreams. We would go on adventures together. It got to the point that I didn't want to be awake.

I thank God that my family was there with me. There was no life insurance policy in place. My husband had just turned 31 years old. He never even pitched in on the household bills. My life was the only one I insured. We couldn't afford health insurance either. If we had, I would have sought out some type of detox and rehab for him. As my pregnancy began to manifest, we found ourselves without any source of income.

I should have emptied my house and removed all the roommates, but I was unable to do so. Their rent was the only thing that was helping us to stay above water. I had to apply for welfare, food stamps, and Medicaid. Even the two safes in the house, which were usually brimming with cash, were nearly empty.

I called and personally visited everyone who loved and cared for my husband, requesting their assistance in covering the funeral expenses. I had zero experience with burying a loved one and was shocked at the cost. I understood that I would need the remaining prudent reserve to support me until the birth of our child.

Every person that I asked gave me a firm, no. His own mother and sister wouldn't even contribute a hundred dollars towards the cost. I decided the only smart thing to do, considering the lack of support I had at the time, was to have him cremated. I did want to have a wake, however, with an open casket. I had attended a wake that featured a blown-up picture of the deceased, and the loved ones expressed that they never felt a sense of closure. Thank God for my parents, who covered 99% of the fees to make this happen, while I covered the remaining amount.

During the few days leading to the wake, people came to my home to pay their respects. One of my roommates grabbed me the day after his death, pulled me into a room, and then locked the door. My other two housemates and Amanda, the girl who had visited the house the previous evening, were waiting for me. They had all been talking amongst themselves and wanted me to have the full picture of what they discovered. Apparently, the last night of his life he had asked for and received Xanax bars from two of them. Everyone who uses heroin knows that you can't take benzos while using opiates. We all remember Donnie, in fact, telling us that several times. So, there was no way that he didn't know the danger. His actions the previous night, the words he was saying to me, and this new information all point to the same conclusion. Did he do this on purpose? He was clearly saying his goodbyes the night before he passed. He would never have taken Xanax bars with a shot of heroin. Our friends, who were sitting on my floor, reported that he had said his goodbyes to each of them.

I firmly instructed them not to disclose this information to anyone. I did not want his mother or sister to hear that he might have taken his own life on purpose. It was clear to everyone who knew him that he was a very depressed and unhappy person. As evidenced by the fact that if he was awake, he had to alter his mind. He couldn't just be. On top of that, the car accident had happened less than a week prior, and the police still had the bottle of GHB in evidence. By now they must have also known that he was driving on a suspended license.

During the initial days leading up to the wake, detectives began visiting the house. I was even more confused. Two of these officers approached me, requesting to come in to our house and ask me some questions. Of course, I said yes. At first, I assumed this had something to do with the car accident and the drugs found on my husband. They quickly informed me that was not the case. These were homicide detectives. They explained to me that when a person dies if they overdosed on drugs, the person who sold them the drugs could face prison time for felony murder. They then asked me this question "Don't you want someone to pay for what happened to your husband?" "No," I told them, "I don't want someone to pay. We are already paying."

My former mother-in-law, Sharon, was there when they came. They spoke to her, too. Looking back, I am confident that she fervently desired someone to pay. She needed someone to blame. As I reflect on this over 20 years later, I now have more experience with death and loss. I've observed a consistent pattern: when someone dies unexpectedly, including suicides, the families almost always attempt to assign blame to a theory or a specific individual. Most people don't want to blame their dead loved ones. The person could have hurt many people and lived a life of bad choices, however, after their death, people tend to talk about them as if they were saints. My husband was not a saint. He had destroyed his own life and mine with it.

I had an awareness of how far down my life had been dragged in such a short time. That didn't make me any less sad, though. Even after his death, I still tried to protect the memory of him. I never shared with anyone that I was almost certain that he had taken his own life. Who would that help? The truth would have only hurt his loved ones more than they were already hurting. I protected that secret for decades.

Chapter Twenty-Seven
"Overzealous Detectives & A Coerced Confession"

The ceremony and wake were a beautiful send-off to my husband. One of his friends had an album that he made for the occasion. It had photos of Donnie through the years. Some of them took pictures of him at his gigs in Elvis's attire. The irony wasn't lost on me. Not only had my husband lived his life like Presley, but he also died in a similar way.

Unbeknownst to me, the heroin in Hillsborough County that year was extremely potent, resulting in numerous deaths prior to Donnie's. A week or so before my husband asphyxiated (technically he had rolled onto his back and choked on his own vomit) the Sheriff's office convened a meeting to deliberate on potential actions. A vaguely written statute essentially stipulated that anyone involved in the distribution of a narcotic that resulted in an overdose death could face charges of felony murder. They were instructed to start charging. Most people understood the purpose of the statute, which was to impose longer prison sentences on drug dealers.

I didn't know the dealer in this case. I knew of him; I had been to his house with Amanda. But I didn't blame him for the excessive combination of substances that my husband recklessly ingested. I didn't blame him or anyone else. It happened. It was unfortunate.

But putting someone in prison would not bring my husband back to life. I was already traumatized. I was a shell of the person I had previously been. It was at this time that I was considering taking his advice and moving home with my family. Sadly, I would never get that opportunity.

The detectives kept coming around. I kept sending them on wild goose chases. I believed in my heart that they would eventually drop it and move on to some real crime. My husband's ex-girlfriend and his estranged mother kept on contacting the police. They wanted me to tell them exactly what had happened that night. I was still trying to protect him, though. In a way, I was also trying to protect his memory and didn't want his family to suffer any further. I did not want them to know that everyone who was there believed that he'd done it on purpose. Who would benefit?

I guess the police got tired of being ignored, as evidenced by their constant return. Like a wild animal hunting for its prey, they held onto it and wouldn't let go. Finally, they came by the house and said, "We need you to come down to the station and tell us the truth. Once and for all." I was scared. They even took one of my roommates and sent her to a different police car. She had a warrant out for her arrest with a different county. I felt like they were trying to intimidate all of us. And it worked.

It was strange. They made it seem like it wasn't a request. I asked them if I needed a lawyer and they told me no. I wasn't in any trouble, according to them. His mom was at the house that day, and the detectives asked her to drive me and my other roommate Christie down to the police station.

When we arrived, they put us in separate rooms. They called it an interview; It was more of an interrogation. These two detectives were not nice. They were very hard on me. Each question they would ask led me to believe in the only conclusion that I could. They wanted me to say that the other guy (Brandy's boyfriend) had injected my husband that night. They obviously couldn't prove it. As I previously mentioned, there were numerous occasions in the past where John provided assistance. There were just as many times where he had "hit himself"; meaning that Donnie did his own injection.

I couldn't do it. I was not going to help them put this young man in prison. They grilled me for hours. I started crying. "Just tell us the truth," they kept saying. Over and over, they said that I was not in any trouble. That the only way this was going to blow back on me was if I lied to them. Why didn't I just tell them I was done answering questions? Why didn't I just ask for an attorney? I tried telling them that he injected himself, but they didn't believe me. When they left the room for a minute, I put my head in my hands, and I prayed. Please God help me. What should I do?

When they returned to the interrogation room, I told them what they wanted to hear. Finally, someone could be blamed. I said it was me. Looking back, how stupid could I have been? There was no possible way to prove that anyone other than Donnie had injected himself. I just couldn't let anyone else take the fall for what was clearly an accident. Unless he did it to himself. I believe the cops were quite surprised with my revelation. That is when they finally decided to Mirandize me. Immediately after, they activated the video camera and asked me to repeat what I had just told them. Then shortly after, they sent me home.

My youngest sister's wedding was coming up soon. I was supposed to stand up at her wedding. I asked the detectives if I could leave and go to New York. They responded, "Of course you can." I assumed that was the end of it. They clearly had their sights on arresting John. I had made sure that would never happen. Now it was time for me to heal and mourn properly.

Later that same day, Tony came by to check on me. Many of my husband's friends had been coming over. They all tried to comfort me in their own way. Sadly, most of these guys were total predators; I had to kick them out. Most of them were trying to get physically intimate with me, attempting to take advantage of my vulnerability while I was pregnant and grieving. But not Tony.

Chapter Twenty-Eight
"The Full Court Press & Unwanted Guest"

It was approaching the time that I needed to plan my trip to New York. Not only did I not want to disappoint my baby sister (she had asked me to be a part of her wedding party) but I also desperately needed a change of scenery. I was grieving every single day. I continued to sleep excessively, as it served as my only escape from reality.

My former mother-in-law rarely left my side. I would throw hints at her about me needing my space. She either didn't pick up on my not-so-subtle clues or she just didn't care.

I was not working at the time and had no money coming in, other than the renters in my house. I was unable to cover the cost of airfare for myself and the children. My car was still being repaired, but far from ready. Sharon offered to drive us to New York for the wedding. There just wasn't any other option, so I said yes.

We packed up the kids and our luggage, and we hit the road. She was in her 70s and not in great health. There were times I had to shake her awake and tell her to pull over and let me drive. It was frightening how she could be wide awake one minute and nod out the next. I'm pretty sure it had a lot to do with the morphine pump that was inside of her stomach area. I even drove her to the doctor's office to have the pump refilled once.

On top of that, she was incontinent. You could casually be having a conversation with her, and then suddenly you would get this overwhelming foul smell of strong urine. To make matters worse, the whole time we were driving, she kept asking me what was going to happen to the baby if something happened to me. She clearly wanted the child that I was carrying. I was always getting pressured by her. She gave the "full court press" of an argument as to why she should raise her son's child. I couldn't have disagreed more.

First, my husband couldn't stand her. The only reason she was in our lives before he passed was because I had pressured him to do so. Being a mother myself, I had compassion for her. Every parent makes mistakes. I felt like forgiveness was warranted. I had no idea how wrong I was about her. I wish now that I could have listened and heeded his advice. I would have saved myself a lot of heartache if I had.

Secondly, she was in terrible health. As much as she criticized us for using drugs, she was no exception. While my husband was alive, she had sent him pain pills and Klonopin through the mail. Wrapped inside of a dollhouse, she mailed this package from Wisconsin to Florida after Vickie's wedding. Yes, he was a drug addict. But clearly, she was as well. Sharon was addicted to prescription medications. In addition to the morphine pump, she had other doctors write her prescriptions for Vicodin and Percocet.

We finally made it to New York after being in the car with her for over 24 hours. I wanted to get as far away from her as I could. My parents were not thrilled that I had brought her to this special family event. I had no choice, I explained. So, they opened their home to her.

In the small town where I was raised, my parents had another couple who were their best friends. Jeff and Linda Adams were the sweetest. While growing up, I babysat for them. They were farmers just like our family. They had raised four boys and did a great job of it. About a year prior, they had lost a son. He was in a snowmobile accident. While in the hospital recovering from a broken back, he developed pneumonia and died. I visited this couple every time I returned home. They even came to my sister's wedding.

My youngest sister Kelly had a beautiful ceremony. All our closest friends and family were there. I could tell it was very awkward and uncomfortable for everyone. This was a special occasion. I was a walking reminder of tragic grief and loss. Most people didn't know what to say to me.

The wedding reception was so much fun, especially for the kids. My Rose and Adam danced the night away. They were both drenched in sweat and hardly sat down to take a break. They were so much happier in New York. If I had known what was about to happen, I would have gladly left them there.

When the father of the bride danced with his daughter, there wasn't a dry eye. The entire family surrounded them, all eyes focused on those two. My sister came and grabbed me and the three of us danced together to the songs "Butterfly Kisses," and "I loved her first." It was a joyful occasion, but also a time of grief. My stepdad and sister tried to comfort me as they held me close, and we danced together. It was a beautiful and emotional day.

Chapter Twenty-Nine
"Subpoenaed by a Grand Jury"

We stayed in New York with my folks for about a week. It was a long drive back home to Florida. I'm not sure why, but it seemed to take longer, even though it was the same distance.

Months went by. Sharon spent a lot of time at my house. She was like the unwelcome guest that just wouldn't leave. I didn't have the heart or energy to be rude and ask her to go. It was helpful to at least have transportation. She would let me use her car to go to the store or pick the kids up from school.

Shane also spent a lot of time at the house, he was a dear friend of Tony. He would come by and check on me and the kids. He cooked for us when he knew I wasn't eating. He became a dear friend to me. I opened up to him. It gave me such great comfort to have someone who wasn't afraid to ask me how I was feeling. He didn't get upset when I cried and couldn't stop.

I was at the 7-month mark of my pregnancy. I hadn't even begun to heal. Everything still felt like a bad dream. I would watch movies and cuddle with my kids. Something had clearly changed for them, they seemed scared. Prior to this, my children were confident and well-rounded. I told them every day of their lives that they were special. I would tell my daughter that she was the most beautiful girl in the world, and that I had chosen to have her! And that she was my favorite daughter! I would do the same for my boy. I would tell him that he was the most handsome boy in the world and my favorite son!

One morning there was this loud knock on my front door. I felt the wall shake in the living room. I looked at the clock on my nightstand; it said 6 am. I knew that this was the police. I hadn't ever been in trouble before, but I could feel it. I climbed out of bed. The kids were with me, and one child was clinging to each leg. I opened the front door, expecting to see police uniforms.

I looked out, and there were news vans in my yard and cameras everywhere. There were two men on my doorstep wearing suits and ties. They didn't look like cops; they looked like businessmen. They then said my full name. Followed by "You have been subpoenaed by a grand jury in the state of Florida, for first degree felony murder." (This is not the same as we have a warrant out for your arrest)

I was in complete shock. Months had passed since I last spoke to those two detectives. I didn't kill my husband. I didn't even want him dead. I didn't sell drugs, even though I was the only one with an income at the time of Donnie's death. The medical examiner had determined that my husband's death was an accident. The manner of death was an overdose.

I found out later that a grand jury only hears testimony from the prosecutor's side. They only get one side of the story, and that's the one that the police will provide. These cops were overzealous, to say the least. They were instructed to utilize the statute I mentioned in a previous chapter. They altered the facts to fit their story. The detectives went back and convinced the medical examiner to change the cause of death to homicide and the manner of death to injection of narcotics. Looking back, it seems clear to me that the information I provided was their whole case against me.

This bad dream had just turned into a nightmare. My kids were ripped out of my arms, screaming and crying. I didn't have any family in Florida. Sharon offered to take them in. I didn't want them to go into foster care, even though, upon reflection, that might have been a better situation for them. I had no idea how sick my ex-mother-in-law was, but I was about to find out.

Years later, my kids told me what happened when they lived with Sharon. Every time the news showed my picture she would point out to my kids "See, your mom is a bad person. She killed my son." I suspect she was behind this all along. I knew she had been staying in touch with the lead detective. I had overheard her telling him that she wanted someone to pay for what happened to her son. I believe I know exactly what motivated her as well. Our unborn daughter was her second chance to do things the right way. If she could keep and raise our baby, then she got a "do over" that she would never get with her son.

Sharon knew how to work the system as well. Even before my daughter was born, she was trying to determine her Native American heritage. She was always looking for a handout. With my two kids in her custody, she was able to get food stamps. The various churches she frequented provided a variety of services. They would pay for some of her utilities and give her money and gifts. Rose told me that she would stand them up in front of the church and fake cry, saying "their mother killed my son." as she sobbed. My daughter said it was humiliating. And that was all just a show. This woman was as sick as Donnie had told me she was. Maybe even sicker.

Chapter Thirty
"Facing a Potential Life Sentence"

My precious children witnessed me being handcuffed. I was taken to the Orient Road jail. While I was in booking (this is where they take you before sending you to a jail cell) the first call I made was to Shane. We had made plans for the beach that day. Instead, a potential life sentence loomed before me. If you were to look at the photo from my arrest that day, you would see a shocked woman, her eyes purple from crying. There was desperation written across my face.

I called my parents as well. No one could believe what was happening. Each person I spoke to was in shock. How could this be? Unbeknownst to me, my picture was plastered on the front of the local paper. And it wasn't just my picture either. There were five other photos. This media blitz involved other heroin overdose deaths that had happened around the same time. Most of the others charged were drug dealers, suggesting a widespread investigation. Apparently, there was a sweep. This was the publicity that the sheriffs' office was looking for. They wanted a big media spectacle. Something that would grab people's attention. The message was loud and clear "We will have harsh punishments for people involved in drug overdose deaths."

By this time, they had moved me to the Falkenburg Road jail. Amanda was arrested and charged on the same day that I was. They referred to her as my co-defendant. They had us on a "Keep away" status. I am not sure what they thought was going to happen by keeping us apart. It's not like we didn't have months of freedom prior to this to get our stories straight. Both of us had spoken the truth, and we've seen the results.

The public defender's office couldn't represent both of us. That was a conflict of interest. Thankfully, right away her family hired a private attorney to represent her. Given the connection between our cases, I hoped this would be advantageous for both of us. Unfortunately, the lawyer they hired was from out of town. He wasn't very helpful, as far as I could tell.

One of the inmates had a subscription to the newspaper. It had been around for close to a week before I was able to read the story they had printed. This was the first glimpse I had into the gravity of the situation we were in.

I suspect that the corrections officers were also aware of the situation. Most of the female inmates had blue bracelets on with their picture and ID number. It was the second night of my incarceration that they came by and woke me. They replaced my blue armband with a red one. I had to ask around the pod to find out why that happened. Apparently, this was done to identify the inmates who were at a higher risk of escaping.

I was charged with a capital crime. If I went to a jury trial and lost, I could possibly face a life sentence. They still hadn't even taken the death penalty off the table yet. That's where we were with the case the night that I went into labor.

I had been locked up for almost two months. My only visitors were my dear friend Shane and his new friend Charlene. Apparently, she had known my husband, Donnie, for years. She began writing letters to me in jail, offering her support. She was in school to be paralegal, and she couldn't believe that the cops had gotten away with charging me. It just didn't make sense to her. Plus, she knew my husband personally and knew that he loved me very much. In her eyes, this was a huge injustice.

Since she and Shane were my only support locally, I connected the two of them. Together they researched the law and precedents. They were consistently reaching out to my public defender, who was way overworked and hardly seemed to know which way was up. They cultivated relationships with people in the community. If I was to beat this charge and get any justice, they believed it would have to be with an experienced lawyer. One that would cost lots of money. Money that I didn't have.

As soon as I felt the labor pains coming, I used the phone and called my parents. This was even before I told the guards. I was about to give birth. I was alone and terrified. A part of me believed that once I had her, they would release me to spend time with my new baby. I was such a fool for ever thinking that.

Chapter Thirty-One
"Shackled to a Gurney"

The minute I realized I was starting labor; I was in a panic. Despite being away from my children, I still had my baby with me. I could feel her moving around inside me. I would rub my belly and talk to her. I shared my hopes and dreams with her. I never felt completely alone. But that was about to change.

It was late at night. I went and told the guards. They called for the medical team. I was taken to the infirmary. There they did a pelvic exam. It was determined that I was telling the truth, so they called an ambulance.

Two armed corrections officers transported me to Tampa General Hospital. These were not the kind and caring type of guards. The death penalty was still on the table at this time, and they spoke to me like I was a threat to society. Whatever happened to innocent until proven guilty? The armed guards shackled me to a gurney. Both of my wrists and ankles were cuffed and connected to the metal bed.

While I was laboring, the only visitor that they let me see was my public defender; or public pretender, as I liked to call him. He didn't have a clue as to how to help me. This was an older, heavy-set man. He was clearly uncomfortable with the scene as he entered. He inquired how I was doing, and then he left.

I did not cry; I did not cuss or yell. It was a long, painful delivery. I did the only thing I could think of doing, which was to pray. I begged God to please help me. I asked for His grace and mercy. I felt my husband's presence there with me. I talked to him as if he were right next to me. The hospital staff was probably wondering about my sanity. I couldn't blame them; I felt like I was losing my mind.

Eventually, it was time to deliver. Some may not know this, but Tampa General is a teaching hospital. Besides the two-armed correctional officers, there was a classroom full of students. These people had never seen a live birth. They were allowed to watch me give birth to my baby. I don't recall ever giving my permission or consent. I'm not sure that they even asked me. I felt like I was a caged animal.

I gave birth to a beautiful, healthy baby girl. I gave her the only thing I had to give, which was her name. I was allowed to keep her with me in my hospital room. My public defender told me he was going to try to get me a bail hearing so I could go home with her. The judge denied his request.

I spent 48 hours with my new little girl. I breastfed her. I sang songs to her. I didn't want to put her down. Even though my parents had flown down, they wouldn't let them in. I was only allowed to have three visitors, and I desperately needed to see my two older children. I hadn't touched or held them in months. I was rarely given a chance to speak to them on the phone when Sharon was feeling generous.

I had to invite Sharon to see my kids. Of course, I let her hold the baby. This was her granddaughter after all. I knew my parents were dying to see the new baby as well. The Department of Children and Families came and spoke to me. They wanted me to give custody to my ex-mother-in-law; whom they called the "victim's mother." I wanted to keep her. They basically told me that wasn't going to happen and that I should keep my three children together. So, I agreed. It was either that or a foster home.

Unfortunately, at the time, I didn't know how evil Sharon really was. In the following months, she would write letters to the judge in my case. She would beg him not to release me. She told outrageous lies to every department in the county. She did everything she could to destroy my credibility with one goal in mind: to keep that baby.

Abruptly, at the 48-hour mark, they came and ripped my newborn baby out of my arms. Immediately following, they ordered me to change back into my orange jumpsuit. I was sobbing uncontrollably. They shackled my wrists and ankles with heavy chains. Then they paraded me through the hospital and out to the awaiting transport van. My eyes were swollen and almost completely shut. All I could see through the slits in my vision were shards of bright sunshine.

Chapter Thirty-Two
"Solitary Confinement- Freedom is an Illusion"

They transported me from the hospital to Morgan Street jail. This was regarded as the infirmary at the time. They placed me in solitary confinement. They let me out of the cell for approximately thirty minutes per day. I was a shell of a human being.

I had very little human contact. All meals were brought into the small room. This jail was eventually torn down because it had spotty air conditioning and problematic plumbing issues. The acoustics inside were that it sounded to me like I could hear my baby crying. I had an out-of-body experience and levitated above myself. I had no idea at that moment that what I was hearing were the other women.

The year that I was incarcerated there, they housed most of the HIV population. These women were crying in their cells, and the sound was traveling into mine through the vents. I could not understand what was happening. My body was releasing what was left from childbirth. My head and heart hurt so badly I thought surely, I was going to die. I kept searching around inside the cell, looking for my baby.

Most people probably did spend their 30 minutes showering or exercising. I spent mine on the phone. I kept calling Shane. He and

Charlene had been researching and speaking to local attorneys. They had one in mind. Shane told me that I needed to speak to my parents and see if they would pay the retainer. The lawyer they selected was named Robert Esquire.

I called my folks and asked. I spoke on the phone to my stepdad several times. I knew this was a big "ask", but my life was on the line. Literally. He himself had been involved in a lawsuit. I asked him how he would have felt if no one was willing to help him. My stepdad asked my cousins, aunts, and uncles. He tried to get people to pitch in and help. Most people wanted nothing to do with it. After all, they were all in New York, and I was in Florida. Most of them hadn't seen me in years. They had no idea how this could have happened. I'm sure they thought if I was so innocent, then how could I have been charged with first-degree murder?

Thankfully, my parents have always loved me unconditionally. I could not have survived what I endured had it not been for them. They paid the retainer. It wasn't cheap either. It would have taken me years to come up with that money. And this guy had a hell of a reputation. Even the judges and prosecutors respected him. He was the best chance I had.

Soon after giving birth, the judge granted us a bail hearing. This time he was amenable. I assume that's what having a high-paid attorney brings. Amanda and I were brought to court for the hearing. We were ordered to a 30-day drug program in jail and received a $10,000 bond. On a first-degree murder charge, we paid a thousand dollars to a bondsman, and we were both released.

Sadly, I had no home to go to. They were in the process of a foreclosure on my house in Tampa. While I was incarcerated, my ex-husband came from Oklahoma and had me sign and release those two houses to him. Of course, he lied and told me that he would sell and split the profits with me. That never happened.

I had nowhere to live—no car, no money. I had no husband. I was incredibly shocked and grateful to my husband's old friend Charlene. She had offered to open her house to me. It was a small one-bedroom home in Carrollwood, not far from where Donnie and I lived. There was a pull-out couch that turned into a bed. She was very warm and caring. In many ways, she was the head of the crusade to right this injustice. I thanked the Lord for putting her in my life.

It was several days before Christmas when I was released. I had gone from solitary confinement twenty-three and a half hours per day to total freedom. Well, not really, though. Freedom was an illusion. I had been charged with a capital crime and now was facing a potential life sentence. At least they weren't interested in trying for the death penalty. I was relieved about that.

Charlene and I got along just fine. She was a little bizarre in her own way. She was getting some type of disability income. Her diagnosis was–Fibromyalgia. I had never even heard of that. Back then, most people thought that was a fake disease. She was on all types of prescription medications as well.

Shane was allowed to come over and visit. The three of us had some good times together. When he wasn't working, he would cook meals for us. Even though I had only known him for a couple of months before all of this happened, he was the person that supported me the most. I came to rely on him heavily. He came to jail and visited several times per week. He also made sure that I always had money in my canteen for food and hygiene products. He was truly a godsend. You never forget the people who have your back when you're the most vulnerable. This man loved me when I was at the lowest place of my life and had nothing to offer. What began as a friendship gradually transformed into something more over time.

Chapter Thirty-Three
"An Unexpected Overnight Visit"

Shane and I would take turns contacting Sharon. Thankfully, she was a very greedy woman and would do almost anything for money. At the time, there was no DCF case plan. What that basically means is that if there was the possibility of a life sentence hanging over my head, they wouldn't even grant me any type of visit with my children. Not even supervised ones.

We would bribe her. Shane would offer her cash money, and she would meet us. Sometimes we would meet at the Countryside mall in Clearwater. Sharon would let us spend a couple of hours playing with the kids. The baby, however, was another story. When she had the baby with her, she would hold her the whole time. I could look at her, but that was it. My two older kids clearly needed me. They clung to me as if for dear life. It was years later before they told me of the severe mental abuse they endured at her hands.

I will never forget that it was almost New Year's Eve. Up until then, the visits with my kids were random and brief. We were never alone; she always had to be right there. I had been in a car accident a year prior and got a small settlement. I used this cash to bribe Sharon with an overnight visit. She agreed, under one condition, that the baby would stay at home with her.

I couldn't believe it. This was the worst year of my entire life, and my children's as well, but we were going to ring in the new year together. I had to pinch myself. I felt like this was such great fortune. Maybe my life was about to turn around. It couldn't possibly get any worse. That's what I was thinking.

Charlene was a doll. She left for the evening so that I could have time alone with my kids. Shane stopped by. We all took a walk. We laughed and talked. I kept squeezing them and lifting them up in the air. We stayed up late to watch movies. After Shane went home, the three of us cuddled up closely and slept in Charlene's bed all night and into the next day. I think we were all heartbroken the next morning when it was time for me to return them to Sharon's apartment.

These visits with my kids were few and far between. I cherished every moment we had together. At least I got to see them occasionally during the time they were in her care. However, I could see how scared the kids were. They didn't have to tell me. They were my babies. Call it mother's intuition if you want, but I knew. I didn't have details, but I could sense that something wasn't quite right.

From the time of my arrest, family members and friends from both sides of the family were engaged in home studies. These relatives were subjecting themselves to all types of scrutiny. Some of these were relatives of Jimmy's, and some were related to me.

The first person to make it to the finish line, so to speak, was Jimmy's mother. Her name is Jane. The thing is that she never liked me. I had told her of the abuse I had endured by her son over the years. In her eyes, he could do nothing wrong. On the other hand, I was a total failure in her mind. Not only had I broken up our marriage and taken his kids far away from him, but I had also married a deadbeat drug addict. I couldn't deny that truth.

When the Department of Children and Families visited me that day to discuss Rose and Adam's future, they appeared completely surprised. They likely believed that Sharon was a remarkable woman who unselfishly welcomed unrelated children into her home. That was the biggest lie ever told!

I saw it very clearly by then. I finally understood why my poor deceased husband despised his own mother and wanted nothing to do with her. The judge had sent me copies of the multiple letters she had written to him while I was incarcerated. She wrote lie-after-lie about me. She made accusations that weren't true. It was her hope that I would never get out. It wasn't because she believed I had killed her son, but rather because she desired to have that baby all to herself. And she won! After years of having little to no contact with my third baby and years of her almost destroying my life repeatedly, I finally gave in. I stopped fighting them. Both the guardian ad litem and the DCF case workers felt that Sharon was the best placement for my child. It was through a quick private adoption that she won. She will turn 25 this year and she has never known me.

When the case worker visited me, she informed me Jane had successfully passed all the rigorous checks, and if I approved, they could relocate the two older children to New York to live with their paternal grandmother. These same people were under the delusion that Sharon was half a saint, that's what it seemed like. I wasn't so disillusioned. Yes, I was able to have random brief visits with my kids. But to what cost? This wasn't all about me. I had a choice for the first time since my arrest. I had the chance to choose what was best for my kids.

It didn't matter to me that Jane had never liked me. It also didn't matter that she lived a thousand miles away. All that mattered was my unwavering certainty that she cherished them both. I knew she loved these precious children.

As far as I can tell, she loved them almost as much as she loved her son, and that was a lot. I didn't even hesitate. I said yes, please, and thank you! Soon after that, they put Rose and Adam on a plane to New York State. Now I was free to focus on myself and get out of this terrible mess I was in.

Chapter Thirty-Four
"The Koala Bear Doesn't Drink"

Amanda and I received court orders to participate in an additional substance abuse program during this period. At the time of my arrest, I was just a recreational user; not to minimize what I was doing, but in comparison to those around me. I was sent to an outpatient program in Hyde Park called "the Centre for Women". Amanda was ordered to an intensive inpatient program called Crossroads.

My children were no longer near me; I couldn't see them. On the rare occasion when their grandmother permitted me to speak with them over the phone, we were on speakerphone, and she was actively listening. Everything was at her discretion. If I said anything close to "Someday we will be back together, or mommy is going to fight and get you guys back. Don't worry." Click, and she would hang up the phone. Jane did not want me to get their hopes up. It was my thinking that hope was all we had.

I was attending these group sessions Monday through Friday. I also had one-on-one counseling and random drug screens. To say that I was suffering was to put it very mildly. Doctors diagnosed me with severe anxiety and PTSD (post-traumatic stress disorder). I had panic attacks if I heard sirens or saw a police car. In less than a year I had lost my husband, my home, my kids, my freedom, and my newborn baby.

I don't believe that I would have survived if I hadn't discovered pills. Pain pills and benzos kept me going. The Percocet would numb the pain and help me forget it. The Xanax helped me relax and even sleep at times. Now that my kids were far away, I did everything I could to "not feel."

It was during this time that I began to understand why Donnie was the way he was. He too had a lot of emotional pain. When he was awake, it was always the goal to change how he felt, to alter his mind. Another part of my treatment was getting my meeting list signed. I was required to attend five 12-step meetings each week. It's not like there was someone there in the building to see who signed my list. Therefore, I committed a breach of trust when I asked others to sign my list, instead of attending the meetings. I found out years later that I only cheated myself.

This went on for a few months. Eventually, I failed a drug screen. Of course, they immediately reported it to the judge in my case. He revoked my bond, returning me to jail for a few weeks. The new requirement for my release was that I would have to live in a sober house with other women, until my trial. This probably saved my life.

I had to make phone calls and interviews from jail. It wasn't easy at all. Many of the sober living homes were already full or had people applying who weren't incarcerated. Most people wouldn't even give me a chance. I knew that the judge wouldn't let me back out until I secured this type of housing.

Finally, I was able to get in touch with the owner of the "Koala House." He was the only person willing to come out to the jail to interview me. He told me he had chosen that name because the Koala bear doesn't drink. I thought that was clever. His name was

Tom, and he had long-term sobriety. He spoke my language. He gave me an opportunity but told me he wasn't going to go easy on me. I admired and respected him. I was grateful.

When I was released from jail the second time, Tom allowed Shane to pick me up. If we agreed to go straight to the house and get checked in. Shane was a lifesaver. He even paid for my deposit and the first couple of weeks' worth of rent.

I was required to have a job. I didn't have any skills or previous employment history. Plus, I was facing a first-degree murder charge. I applied everywhere I could think. I put in applications at 7-Eleven, Winn Dixie, Walmart, Home Depot, Kinko's, and Circle-K, but no one would hire me. I did the only thing I knew I could do; I had no other options. I went back to dancing. I found a quiet out-of-the-way club and got myself hired. I knew this wouldn't look good to the court, so Shane acted like I was working for him with his painting business.

We did what we had to do. There just weren't many options, not for me anyway. I was able to work and buy myself food and clothes. I could now pay my rent and even bought myself a used car. If you recall me talking about the friend of Tony's who came to get his stolen camcorder from me? That same guy became our good friend. Bryan went from selling cars on the side of the road to having a small car dealership. Whenever I needed anything related to cars, Bryan was always my first call.

By now Shane and I were in a romantic relationship. It was more than just a superficial attraction. What we had was born of mutual respect and deep compassion. I don't think we were ever in love, per se. We were a true partnership. He was the person that always had my back, no matter what. We were both single parents and loved God. He never judged me. I didn't have to ask him for help, ever. It was almost like he would anticipate a need before I was even aware of it. He would then figure out how to meet the need. More than anything, we were the best of friends. Sadly, I wish we had kept it that way. We all would have been better off.

Chapter Thirty-Five
"In LIMBO"

During this time, I slept at the "Koala house" at night. I went to mandatory meetings with the other ladies in my house. I danced during the day. When I wasn't dancing or meeting my other requirements, I was with Shane.

He was such a sweetheart, but also very poor. Most of his adult life he lived in trailers or campers. I hadn't ever had this misfortune. It wasn't beneath me, but I had never been in that situation up until that point. We searched the surrounding area and found a trailer for me to rent. It was close enough to my work and my sober living house. Best of all, it was cheap and very affordable. This became our little love shack.

I was submitting to mandatory drug screens. They were random. I made sure I attended at least the weekly minimum of 12 step meetings. Work was going well, and I was easily able to support myself. I even started saving money in the hope that someday soon I would get custody of my kids back.

It really stung me. Every time I went to court, there was another delay. They forbade me from visiting my children, and I seldom conversed with them over the phone. My heart was breaking. My body was aching. There wasn't even a DCF case plan in place yet that I could at least work toward getting them back. In fact, we still were holding regular family court cases, but I wasn't a viable option in their eyes. Not if these charges were still hanging over my head.

I was glued to the television. Even when I was at work, I watched every minute of the "Scott Peterson Trial." Now there was a monster. That man truly set out to take the lives of his wife and child. I couldn't miss a minute of it. When they read the guilty verdict, I cried my eyes out! I was so relieved that Lacy and her family got some justice.

I was driving home from work one night and got into a car accident. I'll never forget the faces of the police officers who ran and checked my driver's license. The computer did not display any information about my husband's accidental overdose; instead, it showed a charge for first-degree murder. How in the world could anyone compare what Scott Peterson had done to what happened in our case? Honestly, it's 2024 right now and the famous "Friends" star, Matthew Perry has died in a similar fashion. People who acted recklessly are being arrested. Yet they aren't charging them with first-degree murder!

Every couple of months there would be a court hearing for my criminal case. I would mistakenly get my hopes up, only to get them dropped. Either the prosecutor or one of the defense attorneys would ask for a future court date, and it would be granted. Delay after delay. They were all getting paid for doing their jobs. But this was my life.

Mr. Esquire began taking his depositions. During this time we discovered that the medical examiner had altered his official report after consulting with the lead detective on the case. Some of the things I heard seemed quite unethical.

In addition to that, I didn't get "Mirandized." Not until after I told them my story. The police led me to believe that I didn't need an attorney and that I had to stay in the station and answer all their questions. I had never been in trouble before; how was I supposed to know that I was free to go? I handed them their whole entire case against me. They called it a "confession" in the courtroom. That was not a confession. I was bullied and scared. They grilled me repeatedly. I didn't drive myself. That was 100% an interrogation. I knew they would tell whatever lies were needed to get the outcome they wanted.

My attorney then started negotiations with the prosecutor's office. We were hoping for a plead of manslaughter. He promised my parents that I would never spend a day in prison. I probably had a better chance at an acquittal, but I could not take that risk.

The lowest that both sides were willing to settle for was 3rd degree murder. In the state of Florida, murder in the 3rd degree carries a mandatory minimum sentence of 15 years in Florida state prison. My attorney expressed his willingness to pursue the case all the way to trial. We both felt that if a jury were to listen to the case, there was a better chance than not that I would go free.

My lawyer explained that the problem stemmed from the fact that juries consist of human beings. And those people are fallible. Could we trust a jury of my peers to not judge me harshly? I was a stripper and married to a stripper. My kids were living in a house where drugs were being consumed on a regular basis. There were orgies going on at night; this was a total lie perpetuated by Sharon, the ex-mother-in-law. She told this to both the criminal and family court. What if they convicted me on the basis that they didn't like me or approve of my lifestyle? Was that a risk I was willing to take? Would I bet my freedom on it?

No matter what I faced, I had to. I was the one that put myself in that position. I could have left him many times prior, but I didn't. The only truly innocent people were my children. I could not risk them. I would not jeopardize my possible future with them, just to save face. It was my decision to make, the lawyer advised. I decided it was less risky to plead guilty than to go to trial. I wish I could have known the outcome, but at the time, this seemed like the least risky option. I pled "open to the court"; this meant that only the judge would hear all the facts of our case. There was no set agreement for punishment, but the judge could deviate from the guidelines if he chose to. My fate lay in the hands of one person.

Chapter Thirty-Six
"Judgment Day"

I will never forget that day as long as I live. It was a hot and humid Friday afternoon. I walked into the courtroom with my knees shaking and my hands sweating. We sat together, my attorney and I, and listened as the prosecutor presented their case to the judge.

I had been examined by several types of doctors. They became expert witnesses and testified on my behalf. The consensus was that I was a textbook definition of a "battered wife". Saying no was not in my vocabulary. I had endured over a decade of physical, emotional, and sexual abuse. To me, it all sounded like an excuse. I would have preferred not to play the victim role. They called these "mitigating circumstances."

My lawyer forbade me from testifying. He assumed that I would fall apart under cross-examination. If I had testified, I would have made sure that everyone knew that I loved my husband and never would have purposely tried to hurt him. I spent our marriage and courtship trying to save him.

After listening to all the evidence in our case, the judge asked if he could delay sentencing for one week. He said these were serious charges, and he needed time to review all the facts in the case. This was not a decision he wanted to make hastily. I agreed and was thankful for his consideration.

We returned to his courtroom the following Friday. I had no idea what to expect. I had been regularly attending a local church named "Temple Heights Baptist Church." I had made friends in that community, and they gave me strength. Pastor Wigton led that congregation. I told them the previous Sunday that if I didn't return, then to read the local newspaper. They could figure it out from there. I was too ashamed to tell them what had happened. I wanted them to understand who I really was.

I stood and faced the judge. He said, "I sentence you to 15 months of Florida state prison, followed by three years of probation." Clearly, he didn't think that I killed my husband. He heard every piece of evidence against me. There were no fingerprints, no witnesses, and no forensic evidence whatsoever. All they had was what I told them. The law was clear; a 15-year minimum was mandatory in the sentencing guidelines. I was very grateful that this judge had used his discretion. There were many other people who thought it was too harsh.

The bailiffs stood behind me, their hands clasped. Upon the pronouncement of the sentence, they came up behind me and handcuffed me. Indeed, they had informed me that probation was likely my fate and that I should not be sent to prison.

My lawyer asked them to be let into the holding cell. There were other female prisoners there already. He stood there in his Armani suit, pleading with me. Mr. Esquire said to me "Don't worry, I will have you out on an appellate bond tonight." I told him, "No. Please, just let me go."

The end was finally in sight. I had already done approximately 6 months total in county jail. The judge gave me credit for every day I had already served. It was time now. I desperately needed to get this behind me. There was no fight left in me. Not for my freedom, anyway. The fight could now begin for my two older children. And they desperately needed their mother.

After a few days in the county jail, they transferred me to the women's prison in Ocala. It was called Lowell. This was a receiving center. After processing some women would be sent to work camps or other similar institutions. Amanda and I both stayed there for our entire sentences. Even though we were called "short timers" we were both convicted of a capital crime, murder.

While in prison the judge sent me a letter. Almost word for word it read, "I not only believe that your husband participated in his own death. I believe he may have caused it. However, you pled guilty to a very serious charge, and I had to sentence you accordingly."

B-dorm was the first dorm I stayed in after receiving my sentence. That building housed many actual murderers. My first roommate had killed several children and buried them in her backyard. I must admit I was very cautious around her.

I met the most amazing women while I was housed there. Many of them had endured the most tragic of lives. Some had killed abusive men. Others had accidents that could have happened to anyone. I had two close friends. One of them had killed a man who wouldn't stop abusing her daughter and grandson. The other was barely over 21 years old. She had been driving her convertible. Her best friend wanted to sit on the back edge of the car, to flirt with the company of passing boys. They were struck by another vehicle, and her friend died on the way to the hospital. Both women were full of regret. And both had received very harsh sentences.

I can promise you this: there are much worse places than jail or prison. I held my head high and did my time. I did not let this break me; if anything, it did the opposite. It built my character. I wouldn't be the woman I am today had I not had that experience. I chose not to focus on the fact that I hadn't killed my husband; God knew that that, and only He mattered. I focused more on how reckless I had been. I contributed to what happened. By allowing that lifestyle and those drugs into my home, I played a part. What happened would have happened eventually. There was no way we could continue to live the way we were living and get away with it. I believe we learn more from our own mistakes and life experiences than from anything else.

Chapter Thirty-Seven
"A Trial Visit Turns to Disaster"

I knew my time was quickly coming to an end. I spent my time incarcerated getting right with God again. I had prayed over and for many of these women. The stories they had remained with me to this day. It was time for my release. The guard who escorted me out remarked, "I have seen many women cry coming in here, but never one coming out." I couldn't stop sobbing. I wish I could have taken many of them with me.

Before I was sentenced, I began to prepare for what would happen after this was behind me. We discovered a small house in need of repairs, in Thonotosassa, Florida. My parents once again came through for me. By now I had that foreclosure on my record, from my home in Carrollwood that Donnie and I lived in prior to his death. So, my parents had to cosign for the new loan. They wanted to be sure that I was able to get my children back in the future.

Shane was there waiting just outside the gate. His brother Charles was driving the minivan. He was the only person who came and visited me while I was down, that's a term used for being locked up. He took my phone calls, wrote me letters, and tried his best to pay the mortgage while I was in prison. He wasn't the most consistent when it came to work. He certainly wasn't great with money. But he did his best to stay on top of this whole thing while I was away. Had it not been for him, I would have had nothing to come home to.

He informed me that the house payment was past due, and the utilities were on the verge of getting shut off. I told him not to worry; I was home now. I started back at my old job right away. Within weeks we were back in good standing with all the bills. Shane gave up his trailer and moved in with me. The best part was that during the weekends we would take care of his two little angels. Shelly and Demi were 5 and 7 years old when I first met them. I treated them like my own children. The thing I admired most about Shane was how much he loved his girls!

My probation officer was quite strict. She was tough. She would drop by our house without warning, and we would meet in her office at least once a month. I submitted to random drug screens. Eventually, she became one of my biggest advocates. It was approximately sixteen months after my release, she set a court date and had my probation terminated. I was very grateful to her.

The best part was that DCF had finally provided me with a case plan. There were measurable things, and actions that I could take that would bring me closer to getting my kids. Unfortunately, Jimmy had a head start. He had already completed almost every task on his list and was close to getting custody back. I felt like this was partly my fault. You see, when I was locked up and he came to have me sign papers for those houses in Oklahoma, he also asked me to sign a paper that would negate the permanent restraining order that kept him from me and the kids. He couldn't even visit them or sell those houses without my consent. Given the current circumstances, I felt like I had no choice. I hadn't thought far enough ahead, though. I hadn't considered that there would ever be a possibility that he could get custody of our kids, once I signed that.

I passed a rigorous home study. Each kid had to have their own room; boys and girls could not share the same room. That's why my folks helped with that house. It was perfect for raising children. It was a quiet rural neighborhood and had decent schools.

The first Sunday after my release, I went straight to church. We walked in; the service had already begun. When the pastor saw me, he came down the aisle toward me and embraced me in front of the congregation. He said, "My sister was lost, and now she has returned." I was afraid that these strict Christians would condemn and despise me. On the contrary, they embraced me with warmth and kindness. They made me feel special. It felt like I was coming home. I wish all churches would make people feel that way. After all, we are all sinners and all fall short of the glory of God.

My pastor and congregation stood behind me. He even accompanied me a couple of times to family court. He spoke highly of the person that I had become. We were very involved. We went to service on Wednesdays, Saturdays, and Sundays. We broke bread with all the other families. Shane's two girls were involved in the children's ministry as well.

There were many other requirements on my case plan. If it said that I had to attend five 12-step meetings per week, I would do ten. If it said parenting classes, I would take anger management as well. I went above and beyond every task. Not only did I submit to drug screens with the state, but I also did as many as were asked by the children's department. When the DCF caseworker dropped by, I would offer to pee in front of her right there. She would laugh and say no, just take this paper and go to the lab. I was trying to show her that I was serious. I was done playing games. I was willing to do whatever it took to get my babies back.

I could tell by the judge's reaction that she was not a fan of mine at all. Jimmy had completed his case plan, and she ordered that the kids go visit him for one week in Oklahoma. I thank God that she did that. She could have just granted him custody without a visit first.

I cried many times in front of Ruth, the case worker. I even shared some of the nightmares of abuse I had endured with Jimmy. She made sure that my daughter had her phone number; in case anything happened, before they went to Oklahoma to visit their dad.

On the third day of the trip, we received a call. My daughter Rose was 9 years old, but very mature for her age. When she and her brother were in Oklahoma, there was abuse in the home. Salina, his new wife, endured regular beatings. At first, she didn't want to get involved, and she feared what would happen to her. But she had kids of her own, and she knew this was not a safe environment for children. My daughter befriended her and begged her to tell the truth. Oh, how brave that woman was. She called Ruth and told her everything. That was the end of Jimmy's chances.

Chapter Thirty-Eight
"The End of Myself"

During this period, I was in the fight for my life. I passed every drug screen. I was staying clean almost effortlessly. I attended 12-step meetings regularly. I was also heavily involved in our church.

Not only did I receive home visits from Ruth, but also from the Guardian ad litem's office. The guardian assigned to the case had become dear friends with Sharon; her name was Nancy. I felt like she believed all the lies that my ex-mother-in-law presented. We would go to family court often and she would say she opposed reunification with the mother.

The other families in our congregation suggested that Shane and I should get married. After all, we were technically living in sin. I had the overwhelming desire to be right with God. I needed His help and power if I were to have a chance at redemption. So, we got married. It was a small wedding in the church. The wedding was attended by a few family members and, of course, our church family. My youngest brother, Jonathan, was the best man. He and Shane were closer than most natural brothers, and their relationship span over decades.

Month after month, we would appear in family court. I tried not to let my hopes rise, yet every time we left, I felt the weight of defeat. The family court judge assigned to our case would look at me with disdain in her eyes. She said to me in the courtroom on several occasions, "You're never getting your kids back. You are a stripper and a convicted murderer. There were loads of people using drugs and having sex in the house with your kids in it. No one is giving you custody. It will never happen."

I would have my Bible with me during these hearings. I kept reciting Psalm 27 over and over. It read, "For in the day of trouble he will keep me safe in his dwelling; he will hide me in the shelter of his sacred tent and set me high upon a rock. Then my head will be exalted above the enemies who surround me; at his sacred tent I will sacrifice with shouts of joy; I will sing and make music to the Lord." I was indeed surrounded by enemies. These people were there to crush any hope that I had. These verses gave me great comfort and the courage to keep going.

They say, "It's always darkest right before the dawn". That statement couldn't have been any more accurate. Many months after fighting the system, I received another rejection. I was told no again. I was crushed. I felt like I couldn't go on. Nothing was going to change, that's what I came to believe. I remember calling my baby brother. I told him that I have a court date again tomorrow. If I lose again, then that's it. This is killing me. I am at the end of myself. He tried to comfort me, but no one could.

I arrived early at court the next day. My lawyer came up and told me that we had to go across the street to a different courthouse. I was so confused. "Why," I asked him. He said that our family court judge was out that day and we were going to be heard by the "General Magistrate." I felt panic and overwhelming doom.

We were all seated around this large oak table. There was the DCF case worker, Jimmy's attorney, myself and my lawyer, and the guardian ad litem. It was very quiet in the room. I bowed my head and began to pray. Then the woman spoke, she said "Please explain to me what has not been completed on this case plan?" There was the sound of shuffling papers. Then she asked, "Why doesn't this woman have her kids back yet?" I don't remember hearing the response. It was the quickest hearing ever. She used her gavel and said, "Reunification for the mother."

I was stunned. I didn't dare move an inch. I leaned over and whispered to my attorney "What did she just say?" Then I heard "we object" from the other lawyer. This was the man representing the abusive ex-husband, Jimmy. The judge then said, "You have five days to file an appeal. Otherwise, this woman has waited long enough."

I went home and actively tried not to get too excited. Ruth and I spoke on the phone every evening. Upon her initial assignment to our case, she also believed what she had heard about me. But she had been in my home on many occasions and had gotten to know me well. I had been very open and honest with her. I could tell that she not only trusted me, but she was also secretly pulling for me.

I asked each evening, "Have the appeals come in yet?" "No, they haven't," she said. By day three, I am getting their rooms ready, with new bedding and clothes in the dressers. On day 4 I inquired about the status of the appeal, and once again she responded negatively. On the final day, I contacted her again, and she confirmed that they had indeed arrived that day. I was crushed. How had I let myself believe that things would be any different? What a fool I had been; they were never giving me my children back.

Late the next day, Ruth called me. She said, "Meet me at Tampa airport tonight at 11:14 pm. I am bringing you your kids." I started to fall on my knees. I cried and thanked the God of my understanding. Apparently, this caseworker stuck her neck out and buried those appeals on her desk. She acted like she didn't even see them. Having already purchased the tickets, she proceeded to

New York, collected my two babies from their grandmother, and returned to Tampa with them. Months later she lost her job.

Three years and 64 days, that's how long I was kept from my two older children. Thank God I didn't give up on the last day. I learned to never quit before the miracle happens.

Chapter Thirty-Nine
"Strangers Cried with Me"

I couldn't believe this was happening! I still had hours before it was time to leave. The minutes ticked by slowly, more so than in prison even. I would jump if the phone rang, certain that it might be someone calling to inform me that it had been a mistake. I had been heartbroken so many times. I knew I wouldn't believe it until they were in my arms.

We packed up the car. I had made huge poster boards with bright writing that said, "WELCOME HOME, and WE LOVE YOU ROSE & ADAM!" A friend let me borrow one of those older VHS camcorders; it was big and bulky but did the trick. We had a handful of balloons. I just kept pinching myself on the ride over. Shane had to drive because I was shaking so badly.

Tampa International Airport is like a ghost town at that time of night. It's not even that big or crowded during the day. We stood there holding our signs and balloons. I was pacing back and forth. The coolest thing was the strangers; people kept coming over to ask me who we were waiting for. I opened up and told them "My kids were taken from me. It's been three years and 64 days. Today they are coming home." Men and women, I had never met stood there and waited with me; some of them even cried.

I couldn't believe my eyes. They were both running toward me. They had grown so big. I still would have recognized them anywhere. My babies were back! The three of us stood there just holding each other. We were laughing and crying at the same time. Ruth looked at me and gave me a nod. My kids are grown now, but they still cry when we talk about the decision that woman made and how she stuck her neck out for us.

We went straight to the house from the airport. The next day, they were introduced to their new stepsisters, but on the first night, it was just us. Shane gave us some privacy. I remember it like it was yesterday. I was lying on my bed, and my son and daughter were right next to me. One on each side. We talked and talked for hours. There was nothing uncomfortable; it was as if we were never apart. I've met many men and women who have been separated from their children over the years. I always tell them the same thing: Your kids will always love you no matter what. My two had been with an evil manipulative monster that tried to convince them I had killed her son. Then they lived with their paternal grandmother, she took great care of them; but said to them "Your mom only cares about sex, drugs, and rock-n-roll." You can't tell my children anything about me! They know exactly who I am.

The school year had already begun. The reunification was arranged at the very last minute. I decided at first that I wanted to homeschool them both. I did this for several weeks. Regrettably, the guardian ad litem expressed disapproval regarding the lack of external observers monitoring their progress. So, of course, I went straight to the church and spoke to our pastor.

These people at church not only loved me, but they also cared for me. They were my family in Florida. Not only was Temple Heights a church, but it was also a school. They offered me a job there. In exchange, both kids would get free tuition to a Christian private school. I was elated. The position was as a custodian.

This was not the most glamorous job; I was merely a janitor. However, I was deeply grateful for the opportunity. But, oh, did it have its perks. I got to ride to school and back every single day with my children. Most days, one of them would even eat lunch with me in the cafeteria. I'm not sure how many kids would choose eating a meal with their mom over their friends. My kids were different and had a unique perspective. We had spent years away from each other. We now cherish every single minute we had together.

One day I was cleaning the boy's locker room. There were several sports teams that played at this school. The boys that used the locker room were from ages four and up to 19. The smell in that building was something that can't even be described. I remember trying to hold my breath as I picked up trash and sweaty clothes on the ground. Next, I was scrubbing the urinals with as much bleach as possible. That's when I heard it. I stopped dead in my tracks. Outside there were kids playing; it was recess time. It was without a doubt my daughter's voice, and she was laughing. I dropped to my knees on that filthy floor and began to speak to God, saying "Thank you, Father. Today I can hear my daughter laugh and play."

My two children quickly became very attached to both of Shane's little girls. They were all pretty much best friends. To this day, they are very close. They have never called each other "step" sisters. We were an instant family. Shelly and Rose were thick as thieves; they did everything together. Adam and Demi shared a special relationship, as well. It was a beautiful time in our lives.

Soon after taking the job as the custodian, I found out I was pregnant. We certainly weren't trying for a baby. All the kids were excited. Shane had always wanted a son of his own. His grandmother used to tease him and say "No more split tails" talking about the girls. He made me promise that he was going to have a son. I don't know how, but I knew I was carrying a boy. So, I made that promise to him.

Chapter Forty
"Quickly Falling Behind"

The kids were doing great in school. We attended church together as a family every Sunday and most Wednesdays. I remember my son complaining that we "lived in church." I think that was because the school and church were basically in the same place. Both Shane and I took turns cooking dinner, and Saturdays were for going places.

It was also at this time that my relationship got back on track with my biological father. He and his wife now have a daughter of their own. Aunt Teesha was younger than my kids, my half-sister was their aunt. We took the kids to New York for a visit.

My parents weren't the biggest fans of Shane. They had seen me hurt so many times and were very protective. I started to think that no man would be good enough in their eyes. Even so, they would welcome us with open arms. My youngest brother became very close with my husband. They were more like brothers than in-laws. Each had a brother of their own that they weren't as close with.

We also visited with my biological father while we were there. He had done a good job raising his stepdaughter, Malinda. Also, I could see what a wonderful dad he was to my new little sister. It was obvious that his wife Donna wasn't a fan of mine, she had never been, but during these times, she made her best effort to tolerate me. He loved those grandbabies too. They adored him and called him G-pa.

I was still very close to my youngest sister. After her marriage to Kevin, they had two little ones, a boy and a girl. They had even visited Thonotosassa once, while I was seeking custody of my children. I'll never forget they woke up one morning, and he said he heard a rooster. My sister was making fun of him, saying there aren't any roosters in Tampa. I said, my dear sweet sister, this is not Tampa. We were out in the countryside, surrounded by roosters.

When we returned to Florida, the school year had ended. It was a long, hot summer. I was getting big in my pregnancy fast. I was aware at the time that while in prison Shane had relapsed on his drug of choice, which was crack. He had been honest with me about it. However, once I returned home from prison, it felt as if it had never occurred. I was too far along now to dance. The pressure was on.

I had to put the kids into regular school. I wasn't willing to continue as a custodian, using all those harsh chemicals. Shane still had his painting business, but we mostly relied on my income to support ourselves prior to this pregnancy. In every relationship I had been in, I was always the breadwinner.

By this point, my probation was over. I had completed my case plan with the Department of Children and Families. The case was closed. I was a free woman. Despite my freedom, I was still convicted of murder. No one would hire me; nowhere decent anyway. I assisted Shane with his studies and helped him obtain his license. He was an official licensed painting contractor in the State of Florida. He was very proud of that. He did not do well in school and left in the 10th grade. This was a huge accomplishment for him.

He secured a contract to paint eight houses in the area. These were all for one builder. He had a hard time keeping good workers. Shane was the type of person who started strong with every project but then faded quickly. He would take a draw on a job, usually ⅓ of the total. He would contribute a small amount to the bills, but he would spend the remaining funds on fun items such as 3-wheelers. His entertainment was always high on his list of priorities. I'm not saying this to be mean or judgmental (you can ask the mother of his two girls) it's just my honest observation.

We started to quickly fall behind on the bills. He had a set of weights in our house, that had previously belonged to Donnie, that he kept adding to. He started showing interest in bodybuilding and had befriended some of Donnie's old buddies. When he wasn't lifting weights, he was either working on his 3-wheelers or riding them. He and my brother shared that passion.

Often, I had to pull through for us. He was terrible with money. Moreover, on certain days, he would get out of bed at lunchtime, despite the expectation that he should be at the job site. He consistently shortchanged his workers. The ones that were reliable didn't stick around for long. I would have to call my old "regulars" these men who were infatuated with me. It made my skin crawl. Shane would have me accompany them to dinners and shopping. Once he even convinced me to go on a trip to Orlando with one of them. Fortunately, this individual was married and wealthy; he never attempted to engage in sexual contact with me.

That's how we paid most of our bills during my pregnancy. I became unhappy very quickly. This was starting to feel like my previous marriage. Shane also began relapsing during this period. He would get a check or cash from a job; we wouldn't see him for a couple of days. He was full of remorse each time that happened. I was kind when he returned. My concern was that if I beat him up emotionally, then it would only get worse. I kept praying this phase would end.

Chapter Forty-One
"I had no Soul Left"

I stayed clean almost effortlessly for close to three years. I did attend an occasional recovery meeting but didn't do any of the steps they suggested. I had my family and my relationship with God. I began to convince myself that I didn't have a substance abuse problem; it was just a case of bad luck. I had only just begun to experiment when I lost Donnie. Perhaps I wasn't the same as him after all.

This pregnancy was considered high-risk because I was over the age of 30. During one of their many tests, they informed me that my unborn child may have Down syndrome. I didn't trust doctors; I put my trust in my higher power. I took it easy and kept the faith.

I delivered a healthy, gorgeous baby boy, just as I had promised! On top of that, he was born on his father's birthday. We had considered other names during those 9 months, but once he shared his dad's birthday, we gave him the only name that made any sense, Shane Jr. My husband was elated!

One of the things I have learned now in my many years of recovery is that once the "gorilla is out of the cage" so to speak, we no longer have control. Shane was there during and after delivery. I was then moved to a private room with the baby. He then went home to get some sleep. I didn't see him again after that for a while.

When it was time for me and the baby to go home, I couldn't get ahold of him. Apparently, he had relapsed, and no one knew where he was. I had to call his elderly father. Jerry was a very sweet man. He picked up Adam and Rose and came to the hospital to drive us home. I tried not to let the kids see me cry.

I need to make it very clear that Shane was not the bad guy in all this. He was a wonderful man and never abused me. It can be challenging for two people with substance abuse issues to be married. There were times in our relationship when he was strong, and I was weak. And vice versa. It just happens to be that he was the first of us to relapse. He couldn't have known what was going to happen. If he had, he never would have picked up the drugs again.

Everything went downhill fast from there. The first three months with the baby were perfect; we even went to New York for a visit with the family. My husband and I took separate flights home. I had stayed an extra day with my folks and was contemplating ending our marriage. Shane was quite sensitive to my emotions and felt what was about to happen. He and all the kids were in the minivan and picked me up from the airport. His dad was going to watch all the kids so we could have a night alone. I figured, Of course, why not?

He had reserved a nice hotel for us; it even had a hot tub and pool. It was my first night away from the baby. Shane said to me "Let's party," Looking back, I can't believe how casually I had said yes. I had never smoked crack or done cocaine in my life. Donnie's voice was in my head with warnings. I didn't even hesitate. My resentment had grown significantly during my pregnancy; from going on dates to pay our bills and driving around with my brother looking for him when he disappeared. I held my baby in my arms, even when I slept. I had so much fear and anxiety about losing him since the last baby I had was torn from my arms.

I started drinking heavily after leaving the hotel. I would start with Tequila shots after breakfast when I was cleaning the kitchen. I would drink all day long. In the evening, I would indulge in other substances. Prior to this, I had barely let Junior out of my sight. Now he was either with his Paw Paw or his uncle Charles. My older kids were scared. I would still occasionally go to church on Sunday. I could feel the impending doom, but I just couldn't stop.

I had unknowingly crossed the imaginary line. Anyone who is a real alcoholic or drug addict will understand what I am about to explain. If we look back at our past, there was a time when if we had a significant reason, we could either stop or moderate with very little effort. But at some point, we cross this line. Once we do, we are baffled. We no longer have control. I knew what could happen but still couldn't stop. I begged God to please help me to stop on my own!

My biggest fears came true. My baby had an ear infection. The pediatrician ordered an antibiotic, which I dropped off at the pharmacy on my way home. My intention was to go back later and pick it up. But our minivan broke down on the ride home. I never made it back to the pharmacy. In our refrigerator there was the same antibiotic, the same strength even. It was prescribed for one of the other children. So, I gave that to the baby. Our vehicle wasn't running yet. I probably could have gotten a ride back to get the baby's prescription, but it wasn't my top priority. The pediatrician called the Department of Children and Families and reported us.

Very quickly they came and took the baby. It was all downhill from there. Neither of us could pass a drug screen. I knew the older kids would be taken next. I had a family member drive Rose and Adam to New York to try and circumvent the court. Once all my kids were out of the house, I had nothing to live for. This became the darkest time of my life.

I always say there are much worse places than jail or prison. All the trauma I had endured prior to this was nothing compared to the darkness inside of me. If I was awake, then I was completely loaded. I couldn't have sunlight touching me. The only place I was even somewhat comfortable was in a dark room with blankets over the windows and towels stuck under the door. I had skin, hair, eyelashes, and fingernails. But I had no soul left. I was an empty shell of a human being.

It was during this time that I became homeless for a period. I would have sold my soul for one more hit. It didn't matter what substance it was. Most of the people that I was associated with were also dead inside. We were like real-life walking zombies. There were some individuals I encountered who truly cared about me, but the majority were merely interested in gaining what they could from a pretty girl who was addicted to drugs.

I did whatever it took to stay loaded. For a brief period, I endured sex trafficking as a result. Shane had long since moved on with his life. But it was he that I called when I found a way to escape. He dropped everything and came to rescue me. Thank God I got away.

Chapter Forty-Two
"The Call that Changed My Life"

There were a couple of supervised visits we had with the baby. We even tried for a period to set up an apartment and get the kids back. Unfortunately, we could not stop using drugs and alcohol.

The family court judge ordered my son Adam to live in Oklahoma with Jimmy. They attempted a similar arrangement for Rose, but she was already a teenager. Rose addressed the court and wanted to be heard. I'll never forget how grown up she appeared. The judge decided that she was old enough and mature enough to choose. There were several family members that would have been great options for her. But Rose refused. She said she would rather be in foster care with strangers than leave Florida. She believed that if she remained close by, there was a chance I might survive.

Most of the next few years were a blur. I only remember bits and pieces of it. Looking back, it's like trying to recall a movie that you had seen only once but were only partially paying attention to. I can remember certain people or places. I hope to never truly recall the details of most of it.

Rose got her first job and cell phone when she was sixteen years old. Thankfully we had access to each other that way. My number always changed because I couldn't seem to hold on to a phone, but her number always stayed the same. There were periods of time when she wouldn't hear from me. Then, when I settled down or tried to live normally, I would reach out to her. Overall, though, I was still a mess. I would only occasionally see her. Someone would drive me to Pizza Hut, where she worked, and I would tell her how much I loved her and hug her tightly.

Adam spent his high school years with his father. His dad kept me at arm's length from him. There would be year-long periods when I would just leave him alone. I knew there was nothing good that I could offer him. I couldn't even take care of myself.

Our precious son, Shane Junior, was adopted. When they first took him from us, I thought I could somehow stop what I was doing. We handpicked a neighbor to care for him. She went through a rigorous process to become a foster parent. I was very grateful. Her name was Kendra, and she was a single mom herself. She had a son and daughter the same age as my older two. That's how I met Kendra. Our kids were close friends. Unfortunately, I discovered years later that they were not as kind to my daughter as they could have been. The son would be cruel and tell her "You're going to be a chicken head just like your mother." That's a derogatory name that people use to call women who smoke crack. There was another foster home where the foster dad clearly had a crush on Rose that made her uncomfortable. Thankfully, he never did anything to her.

Eventually Kendra had taken in many other foster kids. One of them was a baby. The newborn, unrelated to our case, died in her care. The other children were taken from her. I know she loved Junior very much and wanted to adopt him herself. The details of why that didn't happen were never shared with me. The only thing I do know is that eventually little Shane was adopted by a single dad. This man also adopted another son and raised both boys in rural Arkansas. I truly believe he gave our son a much better life than we could have at the time. I am a huge advocate of adoption.

When Rose was eighteen years old, she called me. This would be the call that changed my life. She said, "Mom I am pregnant, and I need you!" Since the age of 14, she has been very serious about a young man, one year older than her, named Fred. I had met him only a couple of times. I was over the moon. I was going to be a grandma. If ever my daughter needed me, it was right now.

Prior to this call, I had been on a mission. I was already spiritually dead. I was clearly on my way to physical death, too. I was in a state of resignation. I knew that I would die an alcoholic death; I had come to terms with that. As a matter of fact, I hoped it would come quickly. I believed that everyone would be better off without me. "It's always darkest before dawn."

God has a way of bringing certain people into your life at just the right time. Around this time, I met a man named Edward. We both had a mutual friend, and she took me over to his house one day. The three of us had hung out together. They weren't dating, just friends. Before we left his house, he slipped me his phone number and asked me to give him a call if I wanted to.

Edward was like no one I had ever met before. He was quiet and thoughtful. I was an extrovert; he was an introvert. When I first met him, I had been up partying for days with no sleep. Even in that condition, I could tell that he was special. The best way to describe it would be to say that I "SAW" him. I recognized his uniqueness. According to him, he knew the same thing. I wasn't in the best frame of mind, but he could tell that I had come from a good family and that I was way better than the way that I was living. He wanted to help me.

Chapter Forty-Three
"Rock Bottom"

When I was completely broken and had lost all hope, I had what is called "the gift of desperation." I knew my daughter desperately needed her mother. She and her boyfriend made it clear to me that if I didn't get sober, I would never be alone with my grandchild, not ever.

By this time, I had moved in with Edward. He was very good to me. Unlike the men I had previously known, I couldn't tell what he wanted from me. Most men just seemed to want to get in my pants. However, he was different. There was something very unconditional about the love he showed me. Neither of us was looking for a romantic relationship. He offered me a home, a safe place to live.

The more time I spent with him, the more I began to enjoy being alive. It had been years since I had laughed a real belly laugh. I was also smiling and sleeping through the night occasionally. I was still struggling, though. I would do great for a whole week, then I would have a brief relapse. I finally broke down and asked for help.

Edward helped me. He told me that he would go all in with me. He did some research on my behalf. I had no money or insurance. At the time, there weren't any free addiction services for women in our area. Thankfully, since then they have opened a Salvation Army rehab center for women in Tampa. But at the time when I was trying to get clean, they only had one for men. In 2010, I willingly entered ACTS detox five times. This was a state-run facility. They did not have a lot of resources for someone such as me. When the substances left my body, I became restless, irritable, and discontented. The other patients there were relaxing, watching television, and playing cards. I envied them. I would sit in the corner with my skin crawling, trying to figure out how to control my breathing and facial expressions. I now understand that it is due to me being a real alcoholic/a real addict, this is different than a heavy drinker. I have a spiritual malady. I kept trying to fill this God-sized hole with substances.

I felt humiliated every time I had to return, but I did not give up. With every fiber of my being, I wanted to get sober. I just couldn't quite figure out how to do it. While in treatment, I started attending the 12-step meetings. There was a group of men that came into the center a couple of times per week. They were doing this for free. They shared their stories with us. For the first time in my life, I felt like I heard my story. I could relate to the details of the pain and guilt. These men shared the things that one would never hear a stranger talking about.

There was a man that I will call "Jailhouse George" and "Billy" the man with one leg. They caught my attention. These men had lived the way I had. They had gone to extremes that most people would be shocked to hear about. The best part was that they had found a solution. I believed them. There was no way they could have known the loneliness and despair that they spoke of. These feelings that I had spent years struggling with were precisely what they were describing.

The last time that I was released from detox, I decided to follow their suggestions. Not all of them, but some. I began going to 12-step meetings. I even had a sponsor, but I only called her when I knew she couldn't be reached. I wasn't honest with her at all; I had some serious trust issues. The other thing I started to do was follow these men back to the detox I had just left. That group of guys became my traveling "Home group."

I was clean most of the days of my daughter's pregnancy, just not all of them in a row. I attended meetings all the time. I was what some would call a dry drunk. I hadn't done any of the work. I was literally fighting myself every day to make it to bedtime sober. I learned a valuable lesson during this dry time: abstinence aggravates alcoholism. What that means is if you don't replace a spiritual program of action with your substance, your life will continue to spiral downward. That's exactly what was happening to me.

I went to almost every doctor's appointment with my daughter. Rose was in her last month. I followed her to the exam room. The nurse took her vitals. It became obvious rather quickly that something was wrong. Her blood pressure was sky-high. The doctor informed me that there was something wrong, and they needed to take her to the hospital in an ambulance. They then told me that I would have to meet her there; I wasn't allowed to ride with her.

Immediately, I experienced a flashback to the death of my husband, Donnie. PTSD is a very powerful thing, and you never know when it's going to hit you. My daughter was my whole world. She was my ride or die! That child stood by through the darkest of days, always believing in me. She never threw my past in my face. She was the most forgiving human that I knew. And something was wrong with her.

I began to panic and shake. I walked out to my car. I could not catch my breath. I was trying to figure out how to get the key into the ignition and figure out where this hospital was where I was supposed to meet her. I remember pulling out of the parking lot and driving a short distance. Out of the corner of my eye I spotted some flashing lights. It was a liquor store. My breathing slowed just enough to catch my breath. I knew that was what I needed. I walked into the store and bought a bottle of hard liquor. I drank it on the way to my car and threw it in the dumpster. My warped thinking was I'm a member of a recovery group and can't get caught with an open container in my vehicle.

It worked! The alcohol did exactly what I needed it to do. It sufficiently calmed me, enabling me to fulfill my role as a mother. I can show up for my child. I went to the front desk and got my picture taken and my visitor's badge. The staff directed me to the appropriate floor and room. I then got in the elevator. As the elevator was going up it hit me, "You know what I need? I need one more." What I have learned since then is that once we ingest a substance, we then develop this phenomenon of craving. This only happens to drinkers of our type; meaning people who drink alcoholically. Most people don't ever experience that.

I finally arrived at the correct floor. I walked into the room. My daughter had an I.V. in her arms and straps over her belly. The sound of the baby's heartbeat could be heard loudly in the room. There was a tear rolling down her face as I bent to kiss her on her forehead. I said, "Mommy must run to the store and grab something real quick, but I'll be right back." And I meant it. I'm pretty sure she already knew I was drinking, even though to this day I have never asked her.

I remember leaving and going back to the liquor store. I remember buying another bottle of alcohol. I don't remember anything after that. I was in a complete blackout. Days later, I came back to my senses. There was a picture on my phone and a message from my daughter. She didn't even sound mad at me. Rose said, "I wanted you to know that your grandson was born today. We named him Xavier. And mom, I hope that you're okay."

I looked around to see where I was. I was in a crack house and had no clue how I got there. I hit my knees on that dirty floor, and I begged God to please take my life. Everyone would have been better off without me, especially my daughter. I had been angry at him for years and engaged in a candid conversation with him. I even said, "You saw me God I tried recovery, it didn't work." That's when I felt God speak to me, not in an audible voice. In my spirit, I heard Him say, "You didn't try recovery; you just went to a bunch of meetings."

Chapter Forty-Four
"The 14th White Chip-One Last Shot"

I stayed in that crack house for several more days. I could not close my eyes without picturing what I had just done. I was so ashamed of myself. I had bottoms before, but never like this. I was a disgusting human being, deserving of nothing. This was something I could never take back.

Our literature tells us (Big Book of Alcoholics Anonymous page 21) "He may be one of the finest fellows in the world. Yet let him drink for a day, and he frequently becomes disgustingly and even dangerously antisocial. He has a positive genius for getting tight at exactly the wrong moment, particularly when some important decision must be made or engagement kept." To make it more relatable, I trade out the pronouns when I read them.

This is exactly what happened. I had been "in the rooms" (which means going to different recovery meetings) for close to a year. I was almost two months dry when my daughter had her baby. I spent all that time focused on being there for that special moment, and I blew it. During that year, I collected 13 white chips, symbolic of surrendering to this new way of life or starting over again.

I made one friend during my time attending meetings. This was the first real friend I had made in over a decade. Her name was

Trisha, and her husband was Jay. They were two of the nicest people you could ever hope to meet. She and I both kept struggling. We kept going to meetings and tried to support each other. I will forever be grateful for her and the sacrifices she made. Trisha loved me until I could learn to love myself.

In my desperation, I used my cell phone to call her. I don't remember the conversation because I was in a terrible state. I do know that I must have told her where I was and that I truly wanted to die. She had a sponsor who threatened to fire her if she went to try and help me. Yes, you can get fired by your sponsor in recovery, much like losing a job. Her husband also begged and pleaded with her not to put herself at risk. Who could blame them for feeling that way? I certainly didn't.

A couple of days later, she arrived at the trap house to collect me. I hadn't had any drugs for a few hours, and reality was sinking in. I didn't want to go at first. I felt like it was a total waste of time. I was beyond human aid. I was completely broken and hopeless. I begged her to please leave. Trisha wouldn't go. She had even stopped at Dillard's and brought with her new clothes and underwear. I was still wearing the same thing I had on when I left the hospital days prior. She made it clear that she wasn't going to leave without me. Reluctantly, I got into her car and left. That was over thirteen years ago, as I write this today.

I spent several days at her house, sleeping and crying. I then returned home to my boyfriend with my tail between my legs. The first thing I did was go to a meeting at my home group. A home group is a place where you attend meetings regularly and let people get to know you. I cried with tears and snot coming out of my nose. My head hung low. I was crawling with shame, guilt, and regret. I picked up my 14th and hopefully, God willing, last white chip.

I have learned in my many years of sobriety some really great things. Most importantly, recovery is not a spectator sport. I thought if I came in and hung out with these wonderful people and listened to them, then that alone would make me sober. That was just not the case for me. Recovery is not contagious; you can't catch it. It's also not sexually transmitted; that's supposed to be funny. You can't sleep with an old timer and be cured.

I am a visual learner. I love analogies. I once heard this scenario in a meeting: Imagine you were morbidly obese with high blood pressure and diabetes. The doctor might tell you that you need to do these things or you're going to die. Maybe you will change your diet. But also, you go to the gym and tour the place. Then you decide to join. Now that you have a membership, you head out to buy a cute outfit and matching sneakers. You can go to the gym twice on Monday, once on Tuesday, Wednesday, and Thursday. You can even show up several times over the weekends. If you simply stand around drinking water, or coffee, and watching everyone else working out, I assure you that your health will not improve. It's not enough to watch other people exercise. If you don't pick up the weights and do the work, then nothing will change. It's the same way with recovery! That I could understand.

Prior to reaching my lowest point, I already had a sponsor. However, now that alcohol and drugs had beaten me into submission, I finally surrendered. I started to get hungry for the program. I really wanted to live. I used to be scared when I would relapse that I was going to die. Many people I had previously hung around were dying. But something changed after that last debacle; I was no longer scared of dying. My fear became that if I relapsed, I would have to live! And I couldn't live another minute of my life the way I had been living.

Chapter Forty-Five
"Depression Can't Hit a Moving Target"

My boyfriend, who I liked to call "my man", took my car away from me. He and Rose had a discussion and decided what and how my foundation of recovery would begin. I had undergone numerous detoxifications and even spent a brief period in rehab. None of those things had worked. Over a ten-year period, I received diagnoses from four different doctors: PTSD, major depressive disorder, severe anxiety, and bipolar disorder. I was clearly a mess. I also believed that I would have to be on numerous medications for the rest of my life.

My first real sponsor (I had some pretend sponsors before, women who tried but I wasn't ready) was Sheila. I barely knew her. The thing that drew me to her was her faith. I knew that we had the same higher power. I will be forever in her debt. I know that I was a handful, needing lots of attention. My recovery was a full-time job, not just for me but for her also.

She was a P.A., physician's assistant. She would buy me supplements and shakes for me to drink. Sheila asked me to trust her. Her suggestion was for me to get off all of the meds so that we could establish a baseline. That way we could see more clearly what was really going on. Our literature tells us that we have a spiritual malady, that once we overcome this, we often heal both mentally and physically; I am paraphrasing of course.

Most alcoholics and addicts aren't completely honest with medical professionals. We often try to minimize or omit our substance abuse issues. If I were to guess, I would say that I must have presented as someone with bipolar disorder. Given the combination of substances I was consuming, this is not surprising. I was convinced that there must be something very seriously wrong with me. I hadn't had a good night's sleep in years. I didn't want to speak or be around people. I had a hard time dragging myself out of bed. I had flesh and bones, but no soul left.

I will never forget as long as I live. I attended a Saturday morning women's meeting at my home group with my sponsor. We met several times per week, reading literature and starting the 12 steps. There was a woman who shared. She had maintained long-term sobriety. I had never seen her before or since. I heard her say this "Depression can't hit a moving target." WOW, I thought!

What did that mean? I was less than 24 hours sober, and that was all that I heard from that first meeting. Over the course of the weekend, I couldn't stop thinking about what she had said; depression can't hit a moving target. Depression can't hit a moving target. That was the prevailing mantra, over and over when I was trying to fall asleep. Even when I was awake. I kept reciting it again and again. I kept trying to comprehend what the message was. Recovery is like that. I have picked up so many profound things just while actively listening in meetings. I also found that I can learn from anyone. It doesn't matter if they are male or female, what color they are, what they believe or don't believe. This is a place where people share wisdom on how to live life on life's terms.

On Monday morning, I decided to walk to the gym. I had no car; both my daughter and boyfriend drove me to meetings every day. They took me where I needed to go. They both invested a lot, as did my sponsor. The gym was within walking distance of my house, though. I remember chain smoking cigarettes all the way there. The one near my house was called "Lifestyle Family Fitness." I walked through the door and froze; I didn't know what to do. Months prior, Eddie had gotten me a gym membership, but I hadn't really used it.

There were some young adults working at the front desk. I said to them, "I want to work out but don't know what to do." They smiled at me. One of them said, "Don't worry there is a group fitness class starting in 5 minutes. It's called body combat, and there's an instructor. She will tell you what to do."

I walked into the class. I was completely wearing black clothes from head to toe and stood in the back of the room. The instructor was amazing and full of boundless energy. Body combat is a combination of Thai chi and kickboxing. I was huffing and puffing. I was quite overweight and in terrible health. I remember bending over, trying to catch my breath, and staring at the clock. Could I make it to the end of class? I was determined to do so. I would pause for half a minute and then get right back up and keep going. Sweat was dripping into my eyes. The class was 55 minutes long. I made it to the end. I couldn't believe it. Edward often told me to stop "starting things." He said, "Molly you must learn to be a finisher." That day I had completed a task.

I walked home from the gym. I was smiling from ear to ear. It's hard to explain what that had done for me. Despite my deplorable state as a human being, I experienced a moment of hope that perhaps, just maybe, I could improve. That night, I slept for the first time in years without the need for medication. I woke up early the next day and thought to myself "Depression can't hit a moving target."

I did the same thing that day, the next, and the next. Each time I would enter the gym I would ask the front desk staff "I want to work out, what do I do?" Each day they would tell me the same thing, that there's a group fitness class about to begin, and the instructor will guide me through it. I frequently took "Body pump," that's with weights, "body flow," "Zumba," "Yoga," and of course my favorite "body combat."

When we come into recovery, we are spiritually bankrupt. We are faced with a threefold problem and a threefold solution. The steps helped me mentally. My restored relationship with my higher power helped me spiritually. Oftentimes, newcomers neglect the physical part, though. For me, the physical aspect was crucial. I had used so many different substances that I no longer produced endorphins or dopamine on my own. Exercise did that for me.

No one can take care of your physical health for you. Good health is not something you can purchase. Your man can't do it for you. It's something only you can do for yourself. One of my new gym buddies, a precious retired woman who lived in my neighborhood and was in great shape, informed me that exercise is the highest paying job you will ever have. It pays in dividends that you can't even see, and they are compounded daily.

In addition to depression, I struggled with an eating disorder since my early adulthood. I wanted to thrive in all areas. I began drinking lots of water all day long. I made sure to get plenty of sleep every night. I tried to eat healthier. I made exercise a priority every day. This process helped me to heal in ways that I can't explain. I began to build self-esteem. I started to like myself just a little bit.

Chapter Forty-Six
"Recovery is about Taking Action"

Ninety meetings in 90 days. Get a sponsor; do the steps. Keep coming back. One day at a time. Keep it simple. Don't pick up, no matter what. These are only a few of the many things they will teach you in recovery. Unless I was deathly ill, I went to at least one meeting every day for the first nine years of my sobriety.

The only thing I ever struggled with was step one. And it so happens that they say this is the only step that you have to do perfectly! Step one tells us that we are powerless and that our lives have become unmanageable. I could clearly see the unmanageability. However, I firmly believed that I was powerful. I had for many years been completely alone on the streets doing whatever I had to do just to survive. I often didn't know when I would eat or shower again. I had come to rely on myself. The God of my childhood wanted nothing to do with me; at least that's what I had told myself. I had gone so far in the opposite direction of my own morals that I felt like I was trying to hide from God.

The first four months were the hardest. First, I was completely unemployable. I hadn't worked a job in many years. I had several minor charges during my time in the streets but no convictions, other than the 3rd degree murder. I had no skills. There was no employment history. I felt hopeless. I wondered, did God save me for this? Did I have no future other than to rely on someone else?

Secondly, I was in a state of emotional distress. I couldn't numb my feelings anymore. I felt it all. The loss, the grief, the pain. It was overwhelming to me. I learned that I had to open up in meetings and share what I was going through. For months, it was the same thing—my babies. How could I have let them be taken for me? What had happened to my two youngest children? Were they okay? Would I ever see them again? How could I move on with my life when they were out there somewhere without their mother? How could I have fought so hard for the older ones but not for them? Over and over, I would cry and speak about this in my home group.

The noon meeting had just concluded. I was about to walk outside to have a smoke. I still smoked cigarettes during my first two years of sobriety. There was a man I knew from my home group, but not very well. He followed me out and said he had a suggestion for me if I was open to it. Yes, of course I was. He told me that he worked with children and families that had been separated. He was involved in the court system somehow. He said to me, "Recovery is all about action. This is an actionable step that could potentially assist you. Get a journal, one for each kid. When you're doing okay and not in fear of relapse; pull it out. Tell them how you are feeling and what is going on in your life. Tell them anything you want them to know. Act as if they are right in front of you. Then someday, if they do come back into your life, you can hand them that journal. Instead of saying Mommy missed you and thought of you often, you have evidence. They can actually read and see how much you loved them and how heartbreaking it was to be away from them."

I did exactly that. For many years I would journal to my two lost children. I had pages and pages. There were tears on the paper where I would write. Best of all, last year God brought one of them back into my life, and I was able to give that book to him. This action made me feel less hopeless and gave me something constructive to do with that pain. When it got to be too much, I would close the journals and put them away.

I also shared in those early meetings about not having any job prospects. After another noon meeting, I had an older lady walk up and ask to speak to me. She worked at the Byrd Alzheimer's Research Institute. There was a position available; it was an unpaid volunteer-only position. And was I interested; she asked me. "Yes, of course I was."

My daughter would drop me off and pick me up. I was there either four or five days per week. I oversaw getting an accurate list of previous donors together, for an upcoming fundraising event. I also often filled in at the front desk. No task was too menial for me. I loved every minute of it. I would rush to assist individuals who had mobility issues in getting out of their cars, and I would also attach parking passes to their vehicles. Whatever was asked of me, I would do it. It felt like the whole staff there loved me and my work ethic. They told me that I stood out.

There was an actual paying position opening, and they wanted me to apply. I couldn't believe my good fortune. They even offered to cover the cost of some courses necessary for my career in this field. That's how much they were willing to invest.

I nailed the interview, and all that was left was for me to pass the level two background check. Until now, no one had inquired about my legal background. It hadn't come up. I was just a volunteer. It gave me such a great purpose to go there every day. It didn't matter to me that I wasn't getting paid. I assumed that this was the way people like me secured jobs in the real world.

I was in a total panic. I kept telling my sponsor, my friends, and my family that this was the end. They will fire me as soon as they see that murder charge. People told me not to worry about it. Many years have gone by, and it probably won't even matter. I went and had my fingerprints taken. Then it was a waiting game.

I continued to show up and do my volunteer work. I was working on my steps with my sponsor and had just finished my fourth step inventory. On a regularly scheduled day, I showed up for my shift. My daughter had driven me, and my newborn grandson was in the backseat. The C.E.O. of the company met me out front. He asked me for my security badge. Not only was I not getting the new position, but I was also no longer welcome on their property. I was stunned. My heart dropped. I got back into the car with Rose and began to sob. I was very humiliated!

Chapter Forty- Seven
"The Great Obsession"

Our literature tells us that "somehow, someday he will control and enjoy his drinking is the great obsession of every abnormal drinker" (Big Book page 30). I was certain that I needed to give up the hard drugs. That was obvious even to me. However, alcohol— I couldn't conceive of that. I tried every experiment known to man to prove that I was not powerless. That is how I ended up with those first 13 white chips. It was a process for me.

Without alcohol, I feared my life would be boring and glum. What I learned is that average people break alcohol down into water, sugar, and carbon dioxide. This is not so for the rest of us. Seven percent of the world's population is alcoholic. That's 400 million people. Alternatively, the term "addict" may be more appropriate. Not only are we mentally different from our fellows, but we are also physically different. When we consume the same alcoholic drinks, we possess enzymes that are insufficient in both quality and quantity. We don't process alcohol the same. When we drink, an increase in acetone levels occurs, which initiates the phenomenon of cravings. So, what is the solution? It is to avoid consuming alcohol or drugs, it's the first drink or drug that gets us started.

We have a body that can't process alcohol or drugs normally; we can't stop on our own once we start. We also have a brain that constantly tells us we need to get loaded. The alcoholic/ addict has such a strong sense of euphoric recall. This memory is so intense that despite all the consequences, we sometimes disregard these warnings and choose to "pick up." To "pick up" means to cave in and either drink or do whatever drug it is we are craving.

After hitting my rock bottom, I surrendered. I stopped fighting everything and everyone. I started to listen to relate instead of to compare. I worked to identify with the feelings or emotions when someone else was sharing in a meeting. Formerly, I would compare myself and disregard it because the person speaking was different than I was, or their story was somehow better or worse than mine.

It was in step two that I began to feel some real relief. This step says that we came to believe in a power greater than ourselves, and that power could restore us to sanity. The insinuation initially offended me. They were saying that I am insane. Well, wasn't I, though? Most of us are very intelligent and highly skilled people. However, when it came to alcohol and drugs, I was clearly out of my mind. My own path to recovery was proof of that.

I had voluntarily committed myself to the same detox repeatedly. I could stop using substances, but I couldn't stay stopped. That was the insanity that they were talking about!

Step three was easy for me once I had a clear understanding of step two. I made a decision to turn my will and my life over to the care of God, as I understood him. I was forever trying to arrange everything and everyone in my life. It was time for me to quit playing God; it didn't work. I needed him to be my director, my employer, my agent, and my father. Deep down in every man, woman, and child is the fundamental idea of God. During my recovery, I discovered we tend to overcomplicate things that are not necessary. It doesn't matter if you're Buddhist, Muslim, Christian, or Agnostic as long as you believe there is a power greater than you are. Recovery is all inclusive.

I knew from my experiences that there was no human aid that could relieve me of myself. I had to rely on and trust in God. Our literature tells us that "God could and would if He were sought." It doesn't say God could and would if I believed. It doesn't say that God could and would if I knew who He was. No, it just says that He could and would if He were sought.

I began seeking God everywhere. There was another gal I sat next to in the corner of my home group. Each Wednesday at the newcomer's meeting, we would tell each other where we saw God working over the past week. My God works through people. Therefore, isolation during difficult times can be dangerous and detrimental. In doing so, we tie God's hands.

While working at the volunteer job, I finished my 4th step. Immediately that night, my sponsor showed up at my house, ready to take my fifth step. The 4th is a searching and fearless moral inventory of ourselves. In the next step, we admit to God, to ourselves, and to another human being, the exact nature of our wrongs. For me, this was my sponsor. When at last I finished pouring my heart out to her, Sheila flipped my notebook over on the table. She looked me in the eye and said "Now tell me what's not written in there. She said don't pause, just blurt it out before you can think of a lie. If you don't share that one thing you were going to take to the grave with you; that's the thing you will relapse over."

There was something. I had done a thing that was so disgusting that I was too ashamed of. I assumed that telling someone else wouldn't make a difference. What was the point, I thought to myself. Still, I trusted her. I spit it out. She was obviously right because I haven't had the need to drink or drug since then. The steps are not logical. It doesn't make any sense how or why it works, but it does! I had tried every solution known to man and had no success. That was before I tried the 12 steps.

I spent my hour with God directly after; this is part of step six. We then pull the textbook (our literature) down from the shelf, making sure we haven't omitted anything. I had a list of my character defects that came out of my inventory. We then said the 7th Step prayer together. There was a list of people to whom I owed amends. These were from my resentment list, my harms to others, and my sexual conduct. I then asked God to help me become willing to go forth and clean up the wreckage of my past.

Chapter Forty-Eight
"Jaded & Rightfully so"

I made the dearest of friends while in recovery. I honestly believed that once I got sober, life would be rainbows and skittles. That is not the case. I do know this though; I wouldn't trade my worst day in sobriety for my best day drunk or high.

Like most newly sober individuals, I thought I would have to resist the urge to indulge for the rest of my life. I assumed that's what recovering people did. They just suffered along from one day to the next. That has not been my experience, thankfully! I wish I had made a list in my first year of sobriety of everything I hoped to gain from this new way of life. I can promise that what came from recovery was greater than anything I could have ever dreamed of myself!

I faced significant challenges during my initial four months of sobriety. Life was overwhelming! Even the simplest of tasks seemed daunting to me. I continued to go to the gym every day. I also joined in service work. There was a list on the wall of our home group, looking for volunteers for the "clean up committee." My dear friend Trisha said we should sign up. I wasn't a huge fan of the idea but thought it couldn't hurt. There were Oldtimers, people with over 20 years of sobriety, who had told us that service work will keep you sober!

We started cleaning the building every other Saturday. It was quite fun. Each person had a task, and we would chat and fellowship while we cleaned. After completing our work, we all took a moment to appreciate our accomplishments. I began to take pride in the things that we were doing. Before then, this was just a building where we all gathered. After that, it became my home. I no longer felt like an outsider that didn't deserve to be there. I started to feel like I belonged. They even trusted me with a key to the building. Me, with a key!!

After the frequent detox treatments I experienced in 2010, I began scheduling myself to bring meetings there two to three times per week. I didn't have enough clean time yet to be the lead person. What I did was go to several meetings until I found the people who already had detox commitments and asked if I could join them. Each of them said that they would be delighted to have me join them. I spent several hours per week with spiritual giants. These individuals, predominately men at the time, tirelessly delivered a message of hope to those unable to attend outside recovery meetings. We also visited psychiatric hospitals for outreach. We were everywhere.

Edward was very supportive and opened our home to recovery gatherings all the time in an effort to help me with my sobriety. Our home felt at times like a small treatment center. On any given night, there might be one or two people crashing in our spare bedrooms. We would host cookouts, potlucks, and game nights! My sponsor and all my buddies would come hang out and fellowship. One of the dearest friends I ever made in recovery was Pete. He is one of the coolest, sweetest, goofiest cats you will ever meet! Due to his disability, he was unable to work and would take me to meetings and service commitments. We became very good friends.

Things were tough for Edward and me in the beginning. He was very jaded, and rightfully so. I did a lot of damage during the first two years of our relationship; I had built up his expectations and then let him down. I would continue this cycle of getting his hopes up just to pull the carpet from underneath him. I tried recovery and failed numerous times. All I had actually done was attend a bunch of meetings, but that is just semantics. I think by the time I surrendered; my man had given up. He didn't believe a word I said. He was hard on me those first few months.

Thankfully, I was completely honest with my sponsor! That was the only thing I did perfectly. Looking back, it's likely that I trusted her so much because I had stopped lying to her and to myself. She suggested that I buy some drug screens from the local pharmacy. The deal I made with Eddie was that if he was suspicious for any reason, then I would pee in the cup. And I would do it in front of him, because I did know how to cheat a drug test by then.

Occasionally, when he picked me up from the gym, my face would be extremely red, indicating that I had just completed a challenging workout. Other times it was not so red. He would take one look at me and start seething with bitterness. My day had been going well. Immediately, he would become angry with me, and snap. He would start accusing me that I must have snuck out to get trashed. "I am not a fool," he would say. My heart would just drop. I knew I was getting better; I could feel it inside my spirit. However, due to my past mistakes, he was hesitant to believe me. In the morning, sometimes he would pull his wallet out and count out cash and place it on the counter before me. He would point to it and say, "There, take that money and go get high. You know you want to. You're going to do it eventually, so why wait? Just go do it now and get it over with."

This went on for months. When he was home with me on the weekends, he was loving, kind, and generous. There were days during the week like that as well. Then there were the other days when he would just lose it. My sponsor and I discussed what to do.

She advised me to be gentle with him; after all, I had caused this. She also told me the day would come when I just couldn't take it anymore, and I would have to be assertive. That day finally came.

I was almost four months sober. My man picked me up from the gym. I guess my face wasn't red enough because he started right in on me, even calling me names. I very calmly said, "come on let's go to the bathroom." I sat down and peed in the cup, with him watching. I set the test on the counter, but it hadn't been processed yet. I knew the test was going to be negative, but Eddie didn't know that. I looked at him and told him this, "I know that I have deeply hurt you, and I regret it. You did not deserve that. I wish I could take it back, but I can't. I want to spend the rest of my life being the woman that God intended me to be. If you allow me, I would love to be the best thing in your life! But after today I will no longer tolerate this. I understand that you are jaded; I take full responsibility for that. But what used to be okay is no longer the case."

Edward never treated me like that again. He told me months later that he saw me at that moment. He could see the evidence that I had changed just by the way I carried myself. He knew then that if he didn't start working on himself, he was going to lose me. Not only that, but he would lose the best version of me, one that he had invested so much in.

Chapter Forty-Nine
"A Recycled Phone Number with Profound Messages"

The night that I completed my fifth step, and my sponsor turned over my notebook, I began to weep. I could see the past in black and white. All the years and the damage I had caused stared me right in the face. I wouldn't let anyone treat the people that I loved as poorly as I had treated them.

Sheila had me write out an exercise called the "Ideal Sex Partner." It was not about sex, but rather who you would want to share your life with. I was to identify all the traits that were a "must have"; for me, that would be to love God, children, and helping the less fortunate. The other list was the "must not"; mine was to not be abusive, controlling, or dislike kids. Obviously, those are just a few examples because my list was quite long for both. I stared at that list for days before it finally dawned on me: this was Eddie. I already had this "ideal" man, and I was living with him. In the early stages of our relationship, we were primarily focused on helping each other; he wanted to save me, and I needed saving. He was so different from any man I had ever been interested in. Honestly, he was a square; which I used to associate with boring. But he was my rock, unwavering in his love and devotion. He made me feel safe for the first time in my life.

During the first two years of our relationship, every time I would relapse, he would take me to Metro (this is an urban cell phone company with the cheapest of pay as you go plans) and get me a new number. Additionally, my phones would get misplaced or stolen. It was his intention that bad people wouldn't have my new number. This was a vicious cycle over and over; we would go do this.

As soon as I returned home from Trisha's house after she rescued me from ending it all, he took me directly to the phone company. I'll never forget that day, he said "This is it. This is the last time we waste money changing your phone number." I could tell that he meant it this time. Some of this stuff was getting old. My parents had one of those phone/address books where you would write in your loved ones' addresses and phone numbers. They had to replace it because my number changed so many times that there was no room to write my newest digits.

These were all recycled cell phone numbers, recently disconnected from other struggling individuals. I'm not saying that every Metro PCS customer is an addict or drug dealer. However, almost every street person that I associated with also used the same company. That's why it was not shocking to me that each new number I would get assigned came with its own wrong kind of people. What I mean by that is this: I would get a new number and almost immediately, random texts would start coming. Some would say "Ladies night tonight, come out and drink for a dime" and give the address and details. Or other texts would say "I've got those blues you've been asking about"; that's a reference to an opiate pill that was blue in color. Another text would say, "I got that good hard you want"; that's a reference for crack cocaine. You get the picture. Every new number I ever got from there had these types of texts.

We left the Metro store with my new phone and number. Right away I started receiving texts from strangers. However, these messages were surprisingly unique. I would get a message with a prayer request. I could tell that I was on some type of thread. I'm sure most people can tell sometimes when there are multiple people getting and sending messages through the same text. Many of them would start with "Gents" or "Brothers." There were messages that told me which Bible verses to study that week. And the ones that were prayer requests—I would stop and say a prayer for those individuals.

These new "God messages" would come to my phone at exactly the right time. What I'm trying to convey is that when I found myself in a vulnerable situation, that's when the messages appeared on my phone. I remember one time I had finished doing step work with a new girl that I was trying to help. I had just dropped her off at her sober living house, located in the hood/bad area of town. I was unfamiliar with the area, and this was before the widespread availability of GPS. I was trying to figure out how to get back to the highway. As I glanced down at the dashboard, I noticed my turn signal indicating an upcoming right turn. I looked up, not knowing at first where I was. I looked around outside and saw the road signs. My car was on autopilot, indicating that I was about to turn onto the road where the crack house of my last debacle was. This wasn't intentional at all on my part. I started crying and shaking. I began to recite the Serenity Prayer. Before I could even finish the prayer, it came to me. I knew what to do, so I called Pete. Now usually he would answer and come running. But on this day, he picked up the phone and said I can't talk right now, you'll have to call me later. Then he hung up on me. By now I turned the turn signal off. Right then, one of those uplifting texts arrived in my inbox. It almost felt like God, or God's people were watching over me. They were present during my darkest moments, prepared to provide guidance. Next, I called my daughter, and she stayed on the phone with me until I made it home safely.

When I arrived at our house, I began to cry and thank my higher power. I took the time to reread the messages on the thread. It was then that I decided to save them on my phone as "messages from God." I have had so many spiritual awakenings while in recovery, that I couldn't possibly list them all. This one with the recycled phone number though was such a powerful example to me of how God works and how much He loves us!

Chapter Fifty
"Cleaning my Side of the Street"

Once I had compiled my eighth step list, which included the individuals I owed amends to, it was time to take further action. My sponsor reviewed with me what I was to say. The wording was entirely up to me as long as I didn't say "I'm sorry." That phrase had been worn out. Every person that loved me had heard that too many times already. They deserved better than that. I took the bit in the mouth and prayed for discernment. I was fortunate that I had a sponsor that took me through the steps quickly; the way they did in the pioneering days. My list of amends took close to a year to complete; this is because many people that I had harmed lived out of state. I was on the 12th step by my two-month mark.

Trisha and I were on our way to Orlando, shopping for the day. This was a girl's trip, and we had been looking forward to it. I was very anxious. This was going to be my first attempt at making amends. I remember she was driving, and I was in the passenger seat. I told her how wrong I was to put her in that position when she picked me up from the trap house. I knew how serious and dangerous that was. I thanked her for being such a good friend and showing me how to be a friend just by the way she modeled it. I then asked her this question "How can I make this right with you?" When I looked over, Trisha was crying. She then started apologizing to me. When she asked, is it okay that I apologize too? I wasn't sure, so I had to call and ask my sponsor. I then made her a promise. I said, "If you will allow me, I would like to spend my life learning how to be the best friend to you that I can be."

The biggest resentment that I had was for my biological father. As a matter of fact, that was one of the main reasons that I had never attempted the steps before. They were written and posted on the wall of every meeting I attended. I knew that at some point I would be the one to face him and apologize. I couldn't even conceive of doing this. This bitterness was such a significant component of my identity; if I were to relinquish it, what would remain of me? This anger fueled me every day of my life. There wasn't a day that went by that I didn't feel the pain of the hole in my heart that his absence had created in me. As mentioned in a previous chapter; I remember, as a little girl, throwing coins into the wishing well and blowing out the candles on my birthday cake. My wish was always the same. The one thing I wanted above all else was to know my father.

Not only had he abandoned me as a toddler; he also abandoned me again and again as an adult. I figured out of all my relatives that he should "get it." When I went to prison and when I lost custody of my kids the second time, he distanced himself from me. It would be as if we had never found each other again. My father had struggled with addiction most of his life. I didn't judge him for that. However, as soon as I embarked on the same path he did, he would abandon me again without warning. I want to stop here and say that he is not the bad guy; I do love him dearly, and we have a pleasant relationship today. But this was my perception at the time when I was newly sober.

My daughter was very close to my biological father over the years. She was certainly a grandpa's girl. I was less than two months sober and had made two of my amends already. He was making a trip to Florida, not to see me but to see her and the baby. I told Rose "It's very important for my sobriety that I get to speak to your grandpa while he is here." She loved her mommy very much, so she made the arrangements. Even though she is now in her 30's she still calls me that.

Edward had gotten us some tickets to the "Side Splitters" comedy club in Tampa. I invited my father to come with me. We went alone because my man knew what I needed to do during this visit. We were in the rental car, and he was driving. My sponsor had prepared me for the worst possible scenario. She told me that this was about me cleaning my side of the street. There was a chance that he might not say anything about him or the things that he had done.

It took all the courage that I could muster to humble myself. I was still deeply hurt that my baby sister (we had the same dad but different moms) had the father I always wanted and needed. He was there for every doctor's appointment, every volleyball game and practice. He was always there to comfort her when she was sick or heartbroken. She was and still is a "daddy's girl" We had the same exact father but totally different dads. She got the childhood with him that I dreamed of. This isn't her fault at all. It's just what it is.

I very carefully chose my words with him that night. I told him how wrong I was to choose alcohol and drugs over the welfare of my children. I admitted to him that it must have been frightening not knowing if they were safe or if I was alive. I can't imagine the pain he had endured. Furthermore, I'm confident that he felt embarrassed when people inquired about his oldest daughter. I took full responsibility for all my mistakes. I then asked him this question "How can I make this right with you?" Amend means to right the wrong. He told me quite simply "All I want is for you to be a decent mother to my grandchildren." Indeed, that was precisely what I desired.

We went to the comedy club and enjoyed our evening. Later that year, I went to New York for a visit. He offered to let me stay in his house with him and his wife. I did stay for one night, during which I also intended to make amends with her. She took me into her home. She said she could tell I was different just by the way I carried myself. It went way better than I had expected. My relationship with them is still up and down. I love my father and enjoy whatever communication we share. I can't hate him forever; that would make me a hypocrite. Unfortunately, I turned out just like him. I also abandoned my kids. Who was I to judge? My kids don't hold any resentment against me, so why should I, with him? My children are my greatest teachers. They have modeled for me forgiveness, compassion, and unconditional love!

Chapter Fifty-One
"The Student Becomes the Teacher"

Almost from the first days of my sobriety, my sponsor had me working steps 10, 11, and 12. Some refer to these as maintenance steps. I believe they are more about growth than maintaining.

In step ten, I learn to do a spot-check inventory. What does that mean? Our literature tells us that recovery takes a lot of effort. This is not an overnight matter. The steps were never meant to be "one and done". We must continue to be watchful and on the lookout for our character defects. I practice mindfulness; being more aware of my thoughts, feelings, and behaviors. Here's an example: Let's say that I'm at work and I'm feeling snubbed by a coworker, which is a common occurrence for everyone, even normal people. However, I may start to treat this person with disdain. I often become passive-aggressive in these situations. Step ten teaches me to catch myself, as soon as trouble arises. I then get out my pen and paper. I look at it from the perspective of a mini-fourth step; who do I resent? What is the cause, what part of myself is being affected, and where am I to blame?

In step eleven, I seek through prayer and meditation to improve my conscious contact with God, as I understand him. Praying only for knowledge of His will for me and the power to carry that out. "When we retire at night, we constructively review our day. Were we resentful, selfish, dishonest, or afraid? Have we kept something to ourselves that should be discussed with another person at once? Were we kind and loving toward all? What could we have done better" (Big Book of Alcoholics Anonymous; page 86) Upon awakening, we invite our higher power into our day and ask that we keep away from self-pity, dishonesty, or self-seeking motives. This is a blueprint for living a good life. In recovery, we try to consider what God's will is for us. Even though I don't claim to know what His will is; I certainly understand what God's will isn't. Sometimes it's a matter of just doing the opposite of that.

After making amends with Edward, Trisha, and my biological father, I met with my sponsor. It was a Friday afternoon, and I will never forget what she said to me. Sheila said, "It is imperative that you find another woman right away and take her through these steps!" I almost choked on my own laughter. "Where in the world would I find this woman?" I asked. It just so happens that I was already bringing a meeting in the Town-N-Country hospital on Friday evenings; trying to be of service to those in detox who couldn't get to an outside meeting.

I went to the hospital detox meeting that evening. There was a nurse working there that night that I recognized. He had also worked at the Acts detox, where I had been a client. He was shocked to see me in this "new state." We talked for a while; he thought I was hopeless and might never recover. He was happily surprised. Then he introduced me to a female patient there. I gave her my phone number and told her she could call me when she was released and sent home.

I handed my phone number to many patients prior to that day, but no one had ever called me. I was only seven- and one-half weeks sober but had already finished the steps, except for some of the 9th step amends which took close to a year to complete. Back in the early days of recovery, they took suffering addicts through the steps very quickly; the success rate was also much higher back then. I had accumulated 14 white chips. Who in the world would want me as a sponsor? That's exactly what I was thinking when she called.

Sue Lynn called me the day she was released from detox. In fact, Sue Lynn told me that as she was leaving, the nurse advised her you had better call that girl, she could help you. I was shocked when I answered the phone. She asked me if I would be her sponsor. Most people in the rooms will tell you that it's wise to choose a sponsor with long-term recovery experience. Yes, I was on fire for the program! However, I was aware that there were likely more qualified individuals available for the position. I said to her, "Yes, I will be your temporary sponsor."

Looking back, I don't think I could have made it through my first year of sobriety without Sue. I knew that she was depending on ME! Her life was on the line; this was an enormous responsibility. When I met her, she was 59 years old and believed that her life was over. She had a thirty-year career at a prestigious company and had been drinking and trudging through work all those years. Many members of our home group tried to talk to her about her commitment to me. They advised her what I already knew; she might be better off with someone else. Sue Lynn wouldn't budge; she chose me. We did this together, one day at a time. I still sponsor her to this day.

Every year in November, I pick up a medallion. Then in December, I turn around and give her the same medallion. The saying goes "When the student is ready, the teacher appears." How applicable that was to my life! There were many skeptics in our group (and rightfully so based on my chronic relapsing prior to me doing the work of the 12 steps) that thought this "experiment" with Sue, and I would fail.

We began doing service work together, and I took her through the 12 steps. Eventually, we both acquired our own detox commitments, inviting outside speakers to share their experiences, strengths, and hopes. I became the chair of that committee; TBAIC. These individuals oversaw the organizing of meetings for various institutions, including jails and prisons. We also both made a commitment to our home group and became the general service representatives. Sue Lynn also had a term as the chair of the institution committee. We spent our first five years of recovery traveling the state of Florida, attending area institution conventions. We would stay in nice hotels and loved being involved behind the scenes. I don't think most people know all that goes into making recovery meetings possible all over the world. In sobriety, we truly get to live our best lives ever!

Chapter Fifty-Two
"Finding Joy"

In my fourth month of sobriety, I received my first invitation to give a talk. Yes, I had been consistently sharing parts of my story already, but that was in detox centers. This was very different. A guy from our home group asked if I would come speak at the Salvation Army. Naturally, I agreed. When someone in recovery asks me to serve, I've learned never to say no.

It was a Saturday night, and there were over one hundred people. While some of the clients were required to attend, particularly those in early recovery, there were many others who chose to attend the meeting as well. I was dressed in a combination of a pantsuit and blazer. At the front table were my sponsor, my boyfriend, Sue Lynn, my friends, and my daughter. I was so scared. It was the first and last time that Rose ever came for one of my "talks" she cried when I told the part about the DCF case worker that brought her back home to me. It was too painful; she had already lived it. I was grateful she was there though; she gave me the courage that I needed.

It was just a few months later that Pete and I had secured a new service commitment. There was a local hospital, Bay Care. They had a psychiatric unit, and many of those patients struggled with substance abuse. We drove together that night. When we arrived in the parking lot, two older gentlemen, both with decades of recovery experience, were waiting for us to enter. They walked us into this gloomy-looking sterile room to wait. I remember saying to Pete, "I am not speaking tonight. These two guys will not approve of me or my story." Yes, I was being quite judgmental, but they appeared to be the type of men who had a very high bottom. What I'm trying to convey is that some individuals in recovery face minimal consequences and achieve sobriety with very little effort. This was not my experience. I worried that talking about drugs, instead of just alcohol, or jail and prison might shame me.

There was only one client that came downstairs that night for the meeting. Apparently, it was voluntary. This young lady and her family were told earlier that day that her psychosis was so bad that she quite possibly may have to be institutionalized for the rest of her life. Her name was Joy. I remember looking at her when she walked in and how much she reminded me of myself just months earlier. She had this blank stare, like there was nothing left inside of her.

Pete started to elbow me when she walked in. "You have to do it," he said. He kept whispering loudly that I needed to take charge and be the one to kick off the meeting. Reluctantly, I did. She initially slouched back in her chair, staring into space. Soon after she sat up straight, she was hearing what I said. I could feel her connecting with my story. Once I saw the effect, I gave an unfiltered version of what had happened and what my life was like today. By the time I was close to finishing, she was leaning in and making eye contact with me. I gave her my number after that meeting, and she became my second sponsee; the sponsor is the teacher, and the sponsee is the student so to speak! She is also still sober today, by the grace of God. Just like Sue Lynn she has continued to assist numerous other men and women.

Months later, Joy told me what had happened leading to her hospitalization. She was married and had two small children. Their house caught fire, resulting in the loss of everything they owned.

She never felt a connection to anyone. She was broken and devoid of all emotions. They had been using heroin for days on end. A few days prior to the incident, her daughter was staring at the television and eating a honey bun, which was a common meal for the kids. She asked her daughter if she wanted to go live with the family. With a tear streaming down her face, the daughter shook her head to indicate, yes. By some miracle, Joy placed the kids with a loving family member. That's when this delusion hit her. Joy's psychosis was such that she was searching for her son and daughter and was being forced to do a "Mercy killing." They obviously weren't there. That is when she ended up in the psychiatric care unit.

Today she is one of the best women you will ever meet. She has over twelve years of continuous sobriety. Joy fought and regained custody of her children. In recovery, she remarried an amazing man; she also helped him to get sober, and together they now have a beautiful little girl. This time she bonded and connected with her baby. I am so blessed that God gave me a front-row seat to the miracle that I witnessed transform her life. She was set to be locked away for her adult life, yet today she is FREE in every single way.

I sponsored several other women in my first year of sobriety. These were just two examples of the radical life change that's available to us all. The cost of this freedom? The destruction of our egos. We must come to the end of ourselves and place our reliance on a higher power. It doesn't matter to me who or what you believe. As long as you believe in something, and it can't be in yourself.

Chapter Fifty-Three
"Daddy's Girl"

What many people refer to as good luck or coincidence, I call God. There were so many spiritual experiences I had in early sobriety. It amazed me that the more I sought, the more aware I became. It was like I had been numb or blind. Now my spirit was fully awake.

My daughter and I received an invitation to join my folks in Seattle, Washington, when I was five months sober. I have a bunch of cousins and an aunt that live out that way. Additionally, one of my sisters had relocated to that area and established a family of her own. My baby sister and her growing family met us out there from Alaska. My youngest brother Jonathan came with his pregnant girlfriend as well.

My daughter and I went with my infant grandson. The longer in recovery I've been, the closer we become. It was a very special time for us. Rose was my confidant and my rock. She attended so many 12-step meetings with me over the years. Even though she's not "one of us" (meaning alcoholic) she could probably sponsor someone, that's how deep her understanding of recovery became. Edward was very gracious; not only had he secured plane tickets and a hotel for the 3 of us. He also pitched in on the minivan rental with my folks. The reason that he chipped in was that I would have access to go to meetings while on vacation. My sobriety was, and still is, his number one concern.

We visited relatives I hadn't seen in over a decade. It was like a mini family reunion and I come from a very large family, I have close to 30 first cousins. We ate out at restaurants and toured the city on foot. Even though it was an enjoyable trip, I started to feel on edge. Prior to this, I hadn't been more than a day without going to a recovery meeting. I asked my parents several times if I could please borrow the rental car. They looked at me like I had three heads. "Why do you need to go to a meeting? Haven't you had enough of that life?", they would ask. At the time, my parents resided in North Carolina and my addiction had caused us to become estranged during most of those difficult years. I didn't want to disappoint them or embarrass them.

I tried to just white knuckle it. I kept in contact with my network of recovery people back home in Florida. I was starting to feel anxious. I was overwhelmed with fear; the last thing I wanted was to relapse. I'm sure these feelings were exasperated because I wasn't in the safety of my home. Plus, it's always a little challenging being with multiple family members and personalities all at the same time.

I was wearing my recovery necklace, which I had never taken off before, it featured a symbol on the front. It was a triangle inside of a circle. This is the international symbol of recovery. Many 12-step meetings display this symbol in front of the buildings where we convene. I was in a restaurant with the whole family, and I was trembling. The waitress taking our order took note of me. Later when I excused myself to go to the bathroom, she asked me "Are you okay?" While she asked, she pulled out her own necklace, very similar to my own, and quietly slipped it right back under her shirt. I told her that I wasn't okay. I desperately needed to get to a meeting.

Later she came to deliver the food to our table. When she arrived, she asked me where I was staying. I told her which hotel.

Everyone at our table was quiet as they listened to this exchange. This kind woman took out a sheet of paper with a list of all the meetings that were within walking distance from our resort. To me this was a total "God wink," here I was over a thousand miles from home. I was in a vulnerable state. It was as simple as wearing this necklace. My parents were blown away. "How did she know you are in recovery," they asked.

That evening, when we made it back to the resort, my daughter swaddled the baby in one of those body wrap carriers. So off we went; we walked over thirteen blocks. Most of the way there, it was uphill. When we were almost there, I could see the recovery symbol on the very top of the building, just over the next hill. I began to softly cry with pure relief. I felt safe.

The 12-step meeting that night was highly effective. I couldn't believe how different it was to our meetings in Florida. It was cool to listen to strangers that I instantly felt a connection with. It was like coming home, somewhere I had never been. Sobriety is like that. We are like-minded people. Whenever I travel today, I always try to make it to at least one meeting; you never know what nugget, wise thing or truth, you will pick up. Some may believe that our tragic stories bind us together, but that's not the case. What we share is a common solution. We have found a way out. Our whole purpose is to carry this message to those who are still afflicted. That is our twelfth suggestion.

On that specific day, my sobriety was saved by a necklace. Months later, I was still getting those uplifting text messages. I was coming up on the end of my first year of sobriety. That day, I harbored self-pity, convinced that I would never secure employment. Who in the world would want to hire me? Nothing seemed to be going right, and I was living in a morbid reflection of the past. I was projecting the worst possible future for myself.

Sue Lynn was driving when she stopped at an Amscot in a particularly dangerous area of town.

I was familiar and had scored drugs at the corner many times in the past. I could see the "dope boys" on the corner. It was a perfect storm. She found herself in a lengthy line at the store. My brain was calculating how quickly I could jump out of the car and get exactly what I needed to get loaded. In my mind, I pictured the relief washing over me. At that very moment, my phone vibrated. I read the text; it was a prayer request. For the first time, I started typing a response. I kept writing and pouring my heart out. I told them how many times they had saved my life and what I had been through. I told them I had almost one year of sobriety, and I couldn't have done it without them. I then pleaded with them not to remove me from this thread, as it was evident that I was not the person they thought I was.

Tears poured down my face as the responses began to flow. These were men of God. I was on a whole thread of pastors. God had used a recycled phone number to reach me! I have never met these men in person, but they are still a part of my life today! They continue to check on me and pray for me. We had long phone conversations, and I have watched some of their sermons online.

Isn't God amazing? It doesn't matter if it's a necklace or a new number. When you open your heart and your mind, there is evidence all over the place that God loves and cares for you! I used to be jealous of girls that had great fathers. Today I know that I am a daddy's girl. I believe that God is absolutely nuts about me! Additionally, he is just as nuts about each and every one of you.

Chapter Fifty-Four
"My Special Boy"

When he was young, there were no signs that anything was wrong with my child. Adam was a little bit clingy, but nothing could have predicted what happened. I coddled him in the beginning. I think I was trying to overcompensate with him, for not having his dad. I'm uncertain about the extent of the abuse he recalls, as he was quite young when we left Oklahoma.

After being taken away from me for the second time, the judge ordered him to live with his father, Jimmy. I already knew that he continued to abuse his second wife, and I found it hard to believe that his behavior may have changed since then. It was out of my hands, and I took full responsibility. If I had stayed off the alcohol and other substances, who knows how things would have turned out? I am great about beating myself up and being the target of my own self-hatred. Unfortunately, those feelings aren't productive, especially in recovery. There's a saying that says, "put down the baseball bat and pick up the feather." I try to be gentle with myself today.

According to Adam, the abuse continued both physically and emotionally. He spent some formative years living with his dad and being the target of that anger. He says that he still has flashbacks from his time in Oklahoma. My son did very well in school. All my children are quite intelligent. He was no exception.

We had held him back in kindergarten, so he was 19 years old when he graduated from high school.

His graduation was in May. Adam had qualified for some scholarships to college, and he had completed four years of ROTC; military cadet training and discipline. His dream was always to follow in his father's footsteps and join the military. My son wanted to serve his country. Every branch of the military was trying to get my son to sign with them. The superintendent presented him with an award for perfect attendance. In addition to the honor roll, he had not missed one day of high school. He was an exceptional child.

That was in May; in August of that same year, he became schizophrenic. It was as if a light switch suddenly went off. It started with extreme paranoia. His dad would call and say that his new girlfriend was scared. My son gave her the creeps, and he slept with a sharp knife under his pillow. When I spoke to him on the phone, he would tell me these bizarre stories that were hard to believe.

This incident occurred during my initial months of early sobriety. None of us knew what to do. We had no clue what was going on. This is quite common. Most people with schizophrenia can tell you that the onset is usually college age. Many never get diagnosed; there's a significant number of them that commit suicide before anyone discovers what's going on. The only experience I had personally was as a child. My maternal uncle was in and out of mental institutions. Although I was too young to learn his diagnosis, my memories of him closely mirrored my observations of my son.

My loving boyfriend had great compassion. I begged him to help. I had no funds and still hadn't found employment. He purchased a Greyhound bus ticket for my boy. Right from the first day I could tell that something was clearly wrong. I couldn't pinpoint the issue. At first, Adam came to live with us. I loved having my son back in my life.

One day my daughter and I were watching Law and Order SVU in the living room. The wall of his bedroom was where the TV's back was. It was a Tuesday afternoon, around lunchtime. We live in a quiet, upscale golf community. My son came into the living room in a panic. His voice was trembling, and his speech was racing. I looked at my daughter; we were both scared. He said "Mom the cops are outside, and the reporters are here. They are coming to arrest me. They think that I kidnapped and raped that girl, but I didn't do it. You've got to believe me!"

Every hair on my neck stood up. I looked out across the lawn, and there was no one there. I checked the other windows as well. He was panicking. I could tell he believed it. I watched him walk into the backyard by himself and lay on his stomach on the grass. He clasped his wrists behind his back, as if he were in handcuffs. I had been concerned before this, but at that moment I felt it in my gut—something was very wrong! My spirit was telling me to do something; do it now!

I very calmly grabbed my daughter and the baby, and we quietly told Adam that everything was going to be okay. I said we are going to grab lunch but would be right back. The minute I got in the car, I took my cell phone and dialed 911. Prior to this day, I had concerns that my son might be mentally ill, but I didn't want to involve the authorities. I feared that if there was a record of this, his military dreams would be shattered. But this day was different. I knew it was time.

I remember the calmness of the trained voice on the other line. She asked me all sorts of questions. She asked me if my son was suicidal. I told her no, he wasn't. She asked again, "Are you sure?"

I said, "Yes." Well thank the Lord, I called right when I did because, by the time the paramedics arrived at the house, he had drunk out of a bottle of commercial grade weed killer from the back patio. The timing of the call most certainly saved his life.

It was days before I was allowed to go visit with him. The doctors warned me that he was hallucinating and wasn't himself at all. I asked the question I feared the most, "Is he schizophrenic?" "It was too soon to tell", they said. He had psychosis and heard and saw things that weren't there. I wanted answers. They just kept dancing around my questions.

I sat next to him and held his hand. Every few seconds, his head would jerk in a different direction, like he was listening to someone. I brought him some slippers and pajamas. I tried making him laugh; it didn't work. Finally, he looked right at me and said, "Mom where is my cell?" I told him not to worry; his wallet and phone were safe at home with me. He looked confused and asked again "Mom where is my cell?" I said, "Adam, where do you think you are?" His answer was, "I am on death row, and they are going to execute me, but I didn't do it. I swear I didn't." I hugged him, looked into his eyes, and said "No buddy, you are in the mental hospital. You're not in prison, you're sick." "Oh, thank God!" he said. That was the beginning of Adam's new life. I thought this would break me, but it didn't. My relationship with him today is at the top of my gratitude list. Watching him navigate his own journey has been one of the greatest blessings.

Chapter Fifty-Five
"My Foot in the Door"

My family used to tease me and say that I was the busiest, hardest-working, unemployed person they knew! My schedule was always full, weeks in advance. I loved sponsoring other women; that intensive one-on-one work was very fulfilling. Additionally, Pete, Sue Lynn, and I consistently conducted these meetings in lockdown facilities, often with the participation of others.

One day, we returned to ACTS detox, which was my personal favorite. I felt like it gave hope to the workers there, showing them that some clients will get it. We met this fiery redhead named Rachel! Right from the start, I could see that she was special. She came from a very good family and was loved! While attending college at USF, she had developed a dependence on Adderall. This led her down a frightening road.

Rachel was young, in her early twenties. Her substance abuse had taken her to prostitution and intravenous drug use. She had succumbed to every trauma known to man. Sitting before me was a shell of a human being. Much like me, she had hair, nails, and lashes. But she had no soul left. She followed us from that detox to the recovery rooms. Today she is one of the most remarkable women that I know. Eventually, she went back to college and earned her bachelor's degree. Rachel is a beacon of light in this dark cold world. She has helped run several different treatment centers and helped thousands of people recover!

After I made it one whole year of continuous sobriety, I started to feel invincible. It amazes me how the EGO (Easing God Out) creeps back in. It wasn't a conscious thought; like here I am, God's gift to the people of recovery! My actions then probably suggested that's how I felt. I was the only one that really knew how bad I was, prior to recovery. I assumed if someone as desperate and dead inside as me could get better, then I would be a person that everyone could learn from. Looking back, I cringe when I think of the behaviors I was exhibiting. I'm thankful that I made it through that clean and sober.

A home for veterans asked me to give a talk after I had been sober for sixteen months. The men and women there were very welcoming. I got up to the podium and told my story. After the meeting, this man came up and handed me his business card. He asked if I had a job or was interested in one. Then he said that he owned a treatment center in Florence, South Carolina, and would be opening a second location soon in Tampa. He wanted to hire me. I thought he was full of crap; there are creepy guys in recovery just like in the real world.

That night, after I returned home, Edward conducted an online investigation into him. We were both shocked to see that he was telling the truth. He was the co-founder of a program that only used the Big Book of Alcoholics Anonymous. I met him the next day. He was staying in Tampa and had already set up his office there. We also met with his clinical director. "Mike" and his father had started this rehab and had helped many people. He offered me my first job working in a treatment center! I was elated.

Two days later I was on a plane heading for South Carolina. I couldn't believe my good fortune. Mike put me up in a decent hotel for the first couple weeks of my training. I did not know at the time that he was married to a wonderful woman and had a reputation for being a cheater. He had several ongoing relationships with other women. I found out months later that the rumor was they all thought he was sleeping with me. The staff believed it, and so did many of the clients. That never happened. I was in love with Eddie and hoped to marry him one day.

I showed up in my best clothes, wanting to look professional for my first real job. The other staff members immediately began talking down to me. They said, "Everyone here is a 5. No one is a 10 and no one is a 1." I have learned that many people when they first get to recovery either feel like they are better or worse than everyone else. I believe they wanted each person to feel like they were all equal. Nonetheless, I couldn't have known that.

There were some very good people that worked there but they weren't kind to me. I was there to get trained. The women's director rarely made eye contact; she treated the clients with more respect than she did me. I would try talking to her, I would ask her questions, and even follow her around. When that didn't work, I tried with some of the men that worked there. Literally the only coworker who was kind and welcoming passed away within a month of me starting there.

I would return to Tampa every couple of weeks to recoup. I so desperately wanted this to work. I had no other prospects. My family would listen and comfort me. I would then return to South Carolina. Eventually, they moved me into a ¾ living house with women who had completed the program. It was a total dump, but I didn't care. There were weeks when I worked 70 hours on site, yet the pay remained consistent. The staff were like slave laborers. I made three hundred dollars in cash per week.

My supervisor advised me to spend more time with the staff and less time with the clients. It amazes me that I didn't relapse. I was early in sobriety, working all the time, and being treated like an unwelcome outsider. The greatest thing that came of this was that my EGO was smashed! During my time there, I guided numerous women through the steps, some of whom are still in recovery.

Upon receiving my 90-day review, I was told that I was entitled, likely due to my selection from a speaker meeting and placement in a role I didn't deserve. I had become enmeshed with the clients, and not knowing any better (total lack of training) let some of them do things or talk to people that are against the rules. I was sent home after four months. I will forever be grateful for that experience. What doesn't kill you will always make you stronger.

Chapter Fifty-Six
"Advocating for Adam"

My son was in and out of psychiatric care facilities. In the early days of his illness, he spent more time hospitalized than at home. I was frightened all the time. Talk about being powerless; this was something I had zero control over. During my numerous years of substance abuse, I experienced periods of extreme psychosis. Especially from withdrawals. This provided me with valuable insight into Adam's mental state.

We tried every option known to man. He lived at home; we put him in an assisted living facility. We tried hospitals, psych wards, and group homes. Nothing worked. It was very painful to watch my boy struggle to even want to live. There was constant chatter of wanting to kill himself. I had heard of a program called "Project Return" in Tampa Bay. This required a lot of phone calls and emails. There was even a waiting list. They offered a comprehensive apartment complex that provided cost-effective housing for individuals with mental illnesses. In addition, they had a day program for clients to attend during the week. I thought this might be perfect. He could be with other people like him. It would give him something to do and help keep his brain occupied.

After completing all the necessary steps, Adam was finally able to move into a studio apartment. The staff would come by and give him his medications for the day. They did not administer or observe to make sure he took them. This place was designed to help people become more independent. The idea that he could be self-sufficient and live a fuller life; that excited me! My only real concern was that he was the only person on the property with schizophrenia. I had high hopes anyway.

By this time, I had a new job working at Health Care Connections of Tampa. This was a local treatment center that had a great reputation. It was family owned, and the people that worked there were much more caring than at my previous job! I was very impressed by the clientele. HCC had a contract with the state of Florida for medical and legal professionals. In other words, if a doctor, nurse, or lawyer needed substance abuse treatment, this is where they would go. I loved it! It was my first job as a behavioral health technician. My role was to observe, document, and report behaviors. Much like the other position, I had very little training. It was after I left the company that I took courses in south Florida to get my certification. I went to the Academy for Addiction Professionals. That's when I learned how to be a great tech!

I would visit my son at his apartment when I wasn't scheduled to work. At the time, my grandson and I were very tight. He loved to be with his MIMI; that's what he named me. We would clean his apartment as my son wasn't inspired to do much. We would then take him out for lunch and shopping for whatever he needed. I thought everything was going well. I stopped on my way to work one day because Adam called and said he needed cigarettes. I could tell right away that something was wrong. I asked if he had been sleeping okay. He laughed and said he didn't need sleep. I found out days later that he hadn't been taking his meds at all. It was obvious that he was hearing voices. I told him that I'll be back tomorrow when I have time. My son got very angry with me. "You told me you were going to stay with me today," he said. "No, I didn't. Why would I say that when I am off work the next couple of days?" When I left for work, he was talking to himself and walking down the road.

The very next morning, little Xavier and I showed up at the apartment ready to hang out for the day. My son was gone, and the apartment was locked. I asked the neighbor, but no one had seen him since early afternoon the previous day. I began to panic. The staff at the leasing office let me into the apartment. It was a complete mess, with all his medications conveniently left on the counter. It was clear he hadn't been taking them. His keys and phone were on the table.

When I arrived home, I was beside myself with worry. My daughter did a search and found that my son had been arrested. He was in the Hillsborough County jail. Apparently, he had been up for days, unmedicated. He lost his way and wandered through downtown Tampa during the night, experiencing severe hallucinations. He told me much later that his delusion was that his father was there inside a building and was raping his wife. Adam was trying to save her. He broke into the empty building, drenched in sweat and frightened to death.

The police charged him with burglary. Burglary is the act of entering a structure with the "intent" to commit a crime. I'm sorry but you can't possibly know the intent of a damaged mind such as my boy's. I imagine they took one look at my son and made an assumption. I have known police to be unusually cruel around mentally ill people. I believe they probably thought he was on drugs. This was the furthest thing from the truth.

My son was placed in solitary confinement. There was a period of four months that I had to fight the legal system, during which I lacked any standing. They prohibited all forms of communication between us, including phone calls, visits, and use of the canteen. While incarcerated, he had a psychotic break and has never fully recovered from that. The best thing that happened was that I was sober. Moms and dads who have experienced similar situations will understand what I mean. I was like a Pitbull that no one wanted to let off the chain. Every court hearing assigned to the case; I was there. The bailiff would tell me, "They won't transport your son, and you have no legal standing; he's an adult. This doesn't concern you." The hell it doesn't. This is my very sick child. If I don't fight for him, then who will?

Month after month I would arrive early and stay for the court hearings concerning my son. On several occasions I walked right up in front of the judge; I knew this wasn't allowed. The bailiffs would rush up behind me and try to get me back to my seat. The judge was curious and asked, "Ma'am who are you?" I spoke as quickly as I could, conveying as much information as possible. I also maintained a high level of organization, compiling a comprehensive list of documents that demonstrated my son's severe mental illness. I begged the judge to please help my boy. He heard me and showed compassion. The wheels of justice moved very slowly. The cops should have marched those charges back, but they never did. It was ordered that my son be observed by several doctors.

During this time, I was a wreck. I still went to my meetings and sponsored other women, but other than that, I was falling apart. Each day it got harder to get out of bed. I was mad at God. "How could you let this happen? He is your son too," I would say in prayer. I spent so much time on my knees desperately calling out to Him. I felt the holy spirit speak to me, not in audible words. What I heard was "you go help my other sons and daughters and I will send someone to help your son."

So that's what I did. I kept myself so busy helping others that there wasn't much time for fear or worry. Eventually, they released my son from jail and placed him in an exceptional mental health facility. For years to follow, he received the best quality of care that money could buy. Best of all was that the state paid for it; I was very fortunate. I could never have afforded the care that my son was given. God had done for me what I could have never done for myself!

Chapter Fifty-Seven
"Living Amends"

It was during this time that I began to make "living amends" to those closest to me, they suffered the most. I made sure twice per year to take time off work and fly to North Carolina to visit my mother. I can't imagine what I had put her through over the years. I think about what it would be like if my own children went down that same path! I'm sure she felt terrified and helpless.

Before adopting this new lifestyle, I was a highly self-centered individual–always thinking of myself and what I could get. I grabbed everything I could from life, disregarding anyone who stood in my way. Every day that I get to spend with my mom is special. Recovery has a way of not changing the past, but rather our perception of it. I tried to out "thoughtful" her. What I mean by that is that I would bestow her with sentimental gifts; she's a very caring, generous human being.

Even when I was earning only $300 per week, I began to send checks to my parents in an attempt to repay my debt. I did that for years. I am quite sure that I owed much more, but the time came when she said enough. Some of the debts were high, such as my legal fees and the house they cosigned for that was foreclosed on. My debt, what remained of it, was wiped clean. This is a common occurrence that I've heard people share about in meetings.

The same was true for my daughter, Rose. She hates asking anyone for help. I would search and try to anticipate her needs and fulfill them before she made a request. One time I surprised her with four new tires for her car. She was overwhelmed with gratitude. She and the man she had been dating since she was 14 got married on Valentine's Day the year after baby Xavier was born. My friends and I were able to help them with a nice wedding. There were many times that they lived paycheck to paycheck. They drove old used clunkers. Edward and I helped and even bought several cars for them.

My relationship at home with Eddie was like none other I ever had. Soon after I celebrated two years of sobriety, he proposed to me. He had been a bachelor for many years. I discovered later that when we first met, he was depressed, suicidal, and estranged from God. We began praying together. His life was radically changed for the better, at least that's what he tells me. We were married on Valentine's Day also, my daughter's one-year anniversary! It was a small wedding, but we both took our vows very seriously.

My husband had always shown up for me. He saw me and loved me at my worst. My journey through the steps and recovery grew my character. I became a decent, honest, respectful woman. Neither of us could have predicted the way things turned out. We have now been together for close to 16 years and married for over ten! We have a beautiful life together. This is the longest relationship that I have ever been in with a man who was not related to me. I still get excited when I'm home at night and hear his car pull into the garage. I feel the butterflies in my stomach, and race to the bathroom to check the mirror to see if I look pretty for my man!

My daughter had three more children in my years of being sober. I was in the delivery room for the second baby, Elijah! WOW! I couldn't believe how special that was. I had switched to a different sponsor, Marlene, by that time. She has been sponsoring me for over 12 years. But my first sponsor, Sheila, called me on the phone that day as I was running through the hospital. I had to switch places with the other grandmother who was waiting downstairs with our firstborn grandson, so she could meet the new baby. I was breathless when I answered the call. She had seen on Facebook that my daughter was in labor. I said "Yes, hello. What's up? I'm in a hurry, my daughter is in the hospital and just had a baby!" Then she asked me "Molly where are you?" I repeated, "I am in the hospital, where else would I be?" She said, "Think about it!" I stopped dead in my tracks. You see, I could have missed it all. That phone call reminded me to think about where I had been when I missed my first grandson's birth. Had I kept going down that path, I would have been dead or in prison. It's only by the grace of God that I wasn't.

Chapter Fifty-Eight
"We were Reborn"

Our literature tells us that we were reborn, and that was my experience! It feels like I have lived two separate lives. One was the life I endured and managed to survive. I should have been dead; I've been resuscitated more than a couple of times. I was spiritually dead, and I felt as though it could have been worse. Then there was this brand-new life. Each day that my eyes open is a new opportunity. I had never previously been a morning person. Now, things are different. I've experienced a radical transformation. I get so excited when my alarm goes off. Now I wake up happy and excited. My prayers used to be God, please help me! Now it's changed to please God use me. Who can I help today?

We never have found my "lost child," the one that was taken from me when I was incarcerated. I daydream sometimes that Oprah or Doctor Phil finds her for me and brings me on to the show! My mother has watched literally every episode that has ever aired on television. She even records the shows if she must work. I've spent years bonding with her over these programs.

To this day all my other kids are very close. The two oldest are Rose and Shelly. Shane's daughters are still their siblings. They took the initiative to stay in contact and follow the case of Shane Junior. Rose eventually got in touch with his adoptive dad in Arkansas. I would arrange a rental car for them, and the girls would drive up to spend a few days with their youngest brother. This went on for years.

Shane Sr. and I remained close friends. We both agreed that we should never been married. He spent several years in prison, then he filed for a divorce. Prison changed him. He was a shell of a human being when he got released. He lived in a little RV in a trailer park. We would talk on the phone sometimes. I would stop in occasionally and bring him hot food. He was also in very poor health. He broke his back and even had other issues that the physicians just couldn't figure out. Our conversations were mostly about him wanting to push the girls to get them to put us in contact with our son.

My approach was significantly different from his. We were the ones that messed up. Junior knew he was adopted, and he was developing a relationship with his sisters. His dad even lets the girls stay at their house when they drive up there to visit. I felt like we needed to be patient and let him come to us. I just didn't feel like we deserved or had the right to intrude in his happy life. The man who adopted him had clearly done an amazing job raising him, according to his sisters.

I'll never forget there was a quick trip to Tampa after Junior turned 18 years old. Shane felt like now was the time; he was very persistent with the girls. Thankfully, they weren't listening to us. Rose said to me "Mom, he knows about his parents. He knows that y'all live here. When he wants to meet you guys, he will ask." I agreed 100 percent. Yes, I was also anxious to meet him, but I remained calm and patient, waiting until he was ready. Not everything is about me today. He never visited us during that trip.

Shane Sr was sad and emotional and was trying to blame the girls. He spent years beating himself up and was bitter with himself and many other people. He believed that meeting his son would allow him to move on with his life. He might have been seeking redemption and forgiveness.

On Junior's subsequent trip to Tampa, we each had an opportunity to meet our son. The girls picked up Shane from his RV and they took numerous pictures of them all together. Even Demi and Adam were there. The kids were all together, and their father was the happiest he had been in many years! I too got to see my youngest boy and spent some time with him before he flew back to Arkansas.

Sadly, that would be the first and last time for Shane Sr, though. Soon after returning to his adoptive dad, his father died alone in his trailer. His body wasn't found until days later. According to the autopsy, he had an unknown heart condition. We strongly believe that he was holding on and waiting to meet his son.

Junior came back down for the memorial. It was heartbreaking to witness Junior losing his father after finally meeting him. Today I am blessed with a beautiful relationship with my youngest son. I even gave him that journal I had written to him over the years.

I live a "GET TO" life today. What I mean by that is I've heard people say, "Oh I have to go to work today, or I have to watch the kids, etc." But no, I don't have to do anything. I get to! It's truly by God's grace and a 12-step program that I get to even have a job or be a mom, a daughter, and a wife! None of this is even possible without the help of my higher power!

Chapter Fifty-Nine
"Normies and Earth people"

In the rooms of recovery, we have traditions that protect us and our way of life. We strive to implement the steps and principles in every aspect of our lives. I have found a 12-step program that has solved all my problems! I do not even require medication for the mental health issues that I thought I had. Some people do need to take medicine and there is nothing wrong with that. It is because of our 11th tradition that I will not identify which group I am in. This requires that we remain anonymous at the level of press, radio, and film.

Those of us that share this journey of recovery have ways to identify non-alcoholic or addicted people. We call them "normies" or "earth people." In the past, I have experienced instances when sharing my struggles with a normie has ruined potential opportunities. Some people still look down on us. They might think this addiction issue is a moral one; I assure you that it is not! We are not bad people trying to get good. We are sick people trying to get well! The American Medical Association has determined that we have a disease. If we had cancer or were diabetic, all would feel sorry for us. However, this does not apply to individuals like us. What we have is an allergy—an abnormal reaction to a common substance. As I described in an earlier chapter, once we take a "sip" or a "pill" there is a phenomenon of craving that takes over!

When I was in my first month of sobriety, I met this beautiful "earth person" she was not one of us. Jillian was the same age as me and from the very same region of the country. She was from New York State, in the rural areas. Jillie was very kind and engaging. Yes, I had already made a couple of friends "in the rooms" but we don't spend more than a couple of hours per day in 12step meetings. What are we going to do with the rest of our time? We met at the gym. We would meet almost every day and take group fitness classes together. There were times that we would stay and take an extra class; we really pushed each other.

My new friend was a stay-at-home mom and wife. I was very guarded at first. I had been burnt before. I had made the mistake of not letting someone get to know me before I opened up about my past. Those were painful lessons, so I was slow to share my personal struggles. Jillian and I began to meet outside the gym occasionally. We would grab lunch and bring the boys. She had two sons, both slightly older than my grandsons. I really enjoyed my time with her.

Initially, I gave her the nickname BGB!! This stood for best gym buddy. I already had my dear recovering friends like Trisha, Sue Lynn, Joy, Pete, and Rachel! But this was different; I was stepping out of my comfort zone. What if I revealed myself to her and she judged me? What if, after I told her the truth, she was no longer my friend? I cherished my relationship with her and was very vulnerable. I knew that if we were going to have an honest, authentic relationship, then eventually I would have to tell her the truth.

I'll never forget the first time that we met with another gal from the gym. The three of us were seated in a restaurant for dinner at Ciccio Cali's. Right away, the two girls were discussing what alcoholic beverage to drink. When asked I told them "I don't drink." the other girl said to me "not ever"? Well, that seemed like the perfect moment for me to take a chance. I didn't open up and tell them my story, I just said "I don't drink because I'm an alcoholic. But you can drink whatever you want. It doesn't bother me."

That was the first and last time that lady hung out with us outside of the gym. However, it opened the door for Jillian and me, as she did not look down on or judge me. She was curious and asked me lots of questions. I thought she would reject me or lose interest. It was quite the opposite. Once she knew the basic details, she was impressed. I was believed to be strong and fierce by Jillian!! Not weak and disgusting. There was another lady we worked out with; it is amusing that she turned her nose up at me whenever we encountered each other thereafter. She never looked at me the same once she found out that I was in recovery. I have learned there are two different ways that people will react to that type of revelation. Either they admire the fact that you overcame this enormous obstacle, or they cringe inside every time they see you.

I thank my higher power every single day for my friendship with Jillian! She is always at the top of my gratitude list. I have learned so much from her. She has shown me that there are people in this world who are full of compassion, integrity, love, and grace. Even though we have only been friends for thirteen years, I know we will share the rest of our lives together. I can't picture my life without her in it. She has made me a better person just for being around her.

Chapter Sixty
"Hope Dealer"

There are still many doors that will not open for me because of my felony conviction. For instance, my felony conviction prevents me from pursuing a college degree in mental health or addiction, or from becoming a licensed social worker. Although I could pay and take the courses, the state of Florida would not permit me to register. The state where I live requires a rigorous level two background check for certification. This is a dream I've had for as long as I can remember. Unless I get my record expunged or the governor were to give me a pardon, this is out of my reach forever.

I have been very fortunate up until now. I've had a twelve-year career working in the addiction field. I've worked for four different treatment centers, one of them for over seven years! I achieved certification as a behavioral health technician and eventually transitioned into the role of a recovery coach professional. I started out my career by being a tech. This is always the lowest-paying position at any rehab. I loved it! I would select shifts that required the least number of clinical staff, primarily those that fell on nights and weekends. This gave me the opportunity to invest one-on-one attention in those who needed it. I have "poured into" thousands and thousands of clients over the years. Many of them are still sober and reach out to me on a regular basis.

I finally received a promotion to the alumni coordinator position after nearly six years as a BHT. Prior to this, I would work with clients at the very beginning of their journey. The fact of the matter is that it's much more challenging to stay clean after you are discharged from the treatment center. This meant that I was now allowed to follow their progress after they went home. I would host events where we would all come together and fellowship! It was amazing! I ended up sponsoring many of the women that were previously clients of mine. I still sponsor a few of them today.

Once I took some courses and passed the oral exam, there were three judges asking me questions; I then obtained my certification as a recovery coach professional. This is one of the few available to convicted felons. With my new certification, I gained access to lead large group sessions at the rehab. It was at that point that I felt like I had found my true calling in life. Being part of the clinical team was something brand new and exciting to me! Instead of having a potential impact on one client at a time, I now had a much larger audience. Some of my favorite topics, which were very applicable to newly sober people, were healthy boundaries, communication and assertiveness, credit building, how to write a decent resume, and how to nail an interview.

The treatment center that I loved working for the most was Coalition Recovery Centers. This was not a place like any that I had worked at before. At the time, CRC was the only facility in our area that accepted Medicaid and low-end insurance policies. Most rehabs are money-making machines. Yes, they exist to assist individuals, but some of them primarily cater to the wealthiest, or rather, those who are not disadvantaged. What stood out the most for me was how they treated their staff. When starting out, each employee began with four weeks of paid vacation per year. This is a "heart and soul-feelings" career, and sometimes staff burn out very quickly. They call this "compassion fatigue" and it's very real.

The pay was also much better at Coalition. The two men in charge were very caring but also strict. I respected that the rules were the same for everyone, and all clients knew exactly what to expect. There was no evidence of favoritism, unlike the previous center I worked for where people received different treatment based on their cash pay or higher-paying policies. Treating some clients better than others can inspire entitlement, jealousy, and bitterness, depending on their position. There were other things that were different as well. For many of the clients, this was the last house on the block, so to speak. There weren't any other options for them, not with the lack of funds they had, so these patients were more. "hungry" for the solution. I love it when I see a desperate person who is willing to go to any length to get and stay sober.

Eventually, I was promoted to the position of family coordinator. This was a job that was created, by my boss, with my skill set in mind. I was able to help build it into a real position in the company I worked for at the time. When a client would arrive at the center I would reach out and try to find the "champion." This meant that I needed to identify who in their life was the biggest cheerleader or advocate. It was a brand-new challenge, and I loved it. When we have a loved one struggling with addiction, it impacts the entire family and everyone who loves that person. Most of these people are sitting at home frightened and feeling helpless. I would be the person to listen to them and validate their feelings. If asked, I would also give them suggestions. I've heard many family members complain that in the past they couldn't get in touch with anyone at the rehab where their loved one was residing. This time, a staff member took the time to initiate contact with them. It was refreshing, and I believe I helped many of them through a very painful process. They often expressed their gratitude to me.

Unfortunately, my favorite treatment center closed its doors for good earlier this year. I remember the day they announced it to us in our staff meeting. Some employees got out of their seats and left; others cried. Me... I wept. I did not want to return to the other place I had worked at before. HealthCare Connections had closed when COVID hit. I decided that maybe now was the time for me to write a book. This was a desire of mine from twenty years ago when I was pregnant with Shane Jr.

The way things are right now, even the rehabs are starting to deny applicants who can't pass the level two background check. I know that God didn't bring me this far, just to drop me on my head. I hope and pray that maybe the right person will read this and help make a change. That's how my faith works. I believe that God works through people. Maybe somehow Oprah gets a copy of my book and decides to help? Someone might reach out to Dr. Phil or someone like him, and perhaps they could assist in finding my missing child. I picture another person someone close to the governor of Florida, or an attorney who advocates for felons; taking this information and helping to get my record expunged or a pardon. Maybe none of that happens. Maybe I'm just dreaming with my head in the clouds. Hope is a powerful thing, and I have lots of it. Today I consider myself a "hope dealer"; dispensing encouragement and hope wherever I go! No matter what, I have faith that everything is as it is supposed to be and that there are no mistakes in God's world. I believe that God has me exactly where He wants me and that He can change my circumstances in an instant!

THIS IS NOT THE END. This is the beginning!

I can't wait to see what God has planned next for Molly!

There are two books that were referenced in this manuscript. One was the NIV Holy Bible. The other is the big book of Alcoholics Anonymous.